100 GREAT (

100

GREAT COPYWRITING IDEAS

FROM LEADING COMPANIES AROUND THE WORLD

Andy Maslen

Marshall Cavendish
Business

Copyright © 2009 Andy Maslen

First published in 2009 and reprinted in 2010, 2014 by Marshall Cavendish Business
An imprint of Marshall Cavendish International

1 New Industrial Road, Singapore 536196
genrefsales@sg.marshallcavendish.com
www.marshallcavendish.com/genref

Other Marshall Cavendish offices: Marshall Cavendish International (Asia) Private Limited,
1 New Industrial Road, Singapore 536196 • Marshall Cavendish Corporation. 99 White Plains
Road, Tarrytown NY 10591-9001, USA • Marshall Cavendish International (Thailand) Co Ltd.
253 Asoke, 12th Flr, Sukhumvit 21 Road, Klongtoey Nua, Wattana, Bangkok 10110, Thailand •
Marshall Cavendish (Malaysia) Sdn Bhd, Times Subang, Lot 46, Subang Hi-Tech Industrial
Park, Batu Tiga, 40000 Shah Alam, Selangor Darul Ehsan, Malaysia

Marshall Cavendish is a trademark of Times Publishing Limited

The right of Andy Maslen to be identified as the author of this work has been asserted by him
in accordance with the Copyright, Designs and Patents Act 1988.

A CIP record for this book is available from the British Library

ISBN 978-0-462-09973-6

Designed by Robert Jones
Project managed by Cambridge Publishing Management Ltd

Printed in Singapore by Markono Print Media Pte Ltd

CONTENTS

Introduction   I

The ideas

1   It's not about you (or is it?)   6
2   Remember, you're selling   8
3   Headline idea—your reader is selfish   10
4   The call to action   12
5   Another headline idea—objection handling   14
6   Businesspeople love offers too   16
7   Write as you speak   18
8   Wish you were here   20
9   On the web, it's (even more) personal   22
10   Grammar doesn't matter . . . or does it?   24
11   What not to put on your order form   26
12   Subject lines   28
13   Avoid clichés (like the plague)   30
14   Keep it short   32
15   Shiny, bright, exciting adjectives   34
16   Imagine . . .   36
17   Parting is such sweet sorrow (actually, it's just sorrow)   38
18   Long copy and why it works   40
19   Does your service live up to the copy promise?   42
20   Do you dissolve your worries in a solution?   44
21   Customers or cannon fodder?   46
22   Don't just do something, sit there   48
23   Online copy that grows your business   50
24   (Type) size matters   52
25   I object   54
26   It came from outer space   56

27	How Web 2.0 changes your copy	58
28	The case of the missing case study	60
29	Write more and double your profits	62
30	There's gold on them thar websites!	64
31	Why I hate teams	66
32	"I want" does get	68
33	What do you mean "If"?	70
34	Send your copy by courier	72
35	Tips for powerful emails	74
36	Long words don't always make you sound more intelligent	76
37	Reassuring your online customers	78
38	Have fun	80
39	*That* formula	82
40	Is your copy FAB?	84
41	Southern fried planning	86
42	Give your reader a KISS	88
43	Short or tall?	90
44	Forget impact, go for understanding	92
45	When you don't have time to plan, plan!	94
46	"I just need to make one more change"	96
47	Another headline idea: true or false	98
48	Be different	100
49	Utilize lexical economy, er, I mean use short words	102
50	Almost unique	104
51	Find your customer's pain point	106
52	Another headline idea: use "How . . ."	108
53	We're not selling to *you*	110
54	Give your reader space to think	112
55	Let's play 20 questions	114
56	Optimize for your customer first	116
57	Use storytelling techniques	118
58	Look at me! I'm smiling and pointing at a laptop	120

59	The right way to use numbers	122
60	Ask your reader a question	124
61	You flatter me!	126
62	Your questions answered	128
63	How to go upmarket	130
64	Use pictures your reader identifies with	132
65	Powered by facts	134
66	Selling to international managers	136
67	Skip skip intro	138
68	Satisfy their cravings	140
69	Tailor the message to the audience	142
70	Get a cross-head	144
71	Create curiosity	146
72	Make your ads look like—and read like—editorial	148
73	Watch that hackneyed image	150
74	Correct your prospect's assumptions	152
75	A great golf tournament with a pretty nice conference attached	154
76	Act like a magpie	156
77	Watch your readability	158
78	Say "Hi"	160
79	Grammar *does* matter	162
80	Will wordplay work?	164
81	Use language your customers can understand	166
82	Get them nodding	168
83	Dig down to the underlying proposition	170
84	Yet another headline idea—use "Now"	172
85	It doesn't have to be A4, or A5, or . . .	174
86	Cheese for Christmas?	176
87	Get your customers to speak on your behalf	178
88	How to deal with high prices	180
89	What are they afraid of?	182

90 "Uneven numbers are the gods' delight." Virgil,
        The Eclogues   184
91 Horses beat camels   186
92 Befriend a designer   188
93 Use personal data intelligently   190
94 Start your sentences with And. Or don't   192
95 Boring for whom?   194
96 Create a questionnaire   196
97 Give people a glimpse behind the scenes   198
98 Tap into people's aspirations   200
99 Follow the law of gravity   202
100 Get to know people   204

Afterword   207

INTRODUCTION

Where face-to-face selling isn't an option—because your total pool of prospects is too big or geographically dispersed, or you don't have the budget for a salesforce, or it just doesn't fit with your business model—the answer is copywriting.

I wrote my first sales copy in May 1986. It was for a market research report. I had to write a direct mail pack consisting of a two-sided A4 sales letter and a four-page A4 brochure. There was also a press release, I seem to remember. Oh, and a catalog entry. No web copy—that wasn't invented then. Nor, in any real sense, were PCs. So I wrote my copy longhand on lined paper with a rather beautiful Waterman fountain pen. For younger readers, a fountain pen is a sort of metal tube filled with liquid ink (not toner) and tipped with a little piece of gold-plated steel that squirts the ink onto a piece of paper. Once I had finished my first draft, I handed it to the Marketing Department secretary—Pauline—and she went off to type it up on . . . the computer. You could tell when Pauline switched the computer on because all the lights dimmed and an unearthly humming permeated the building.

Some time later Pauline would turn up again with the copy, now printed in Courier 12 point on crisp sheets of white paper. I'd read it over, make a few edits, and hand it back to P—who'd repeat the whole process until I was happy.

Nowadays I write my copy on a PC or, occasionally, a laptop, as I suppose you do. But although the *technology* I use to write copy has changed, the *techniques* I use are the same as they were in May 1986. I still write plans before writing copy. I still try to figure out what my reader wants to hear, rather than what I want to write. I still make a list of all the ways the product I'm selling benefits the reader. And I still use the old standby AIDCA (see Idea 39). What has changed, for the better, is my skill in *using* the techniques.

I reckon I've written somewhere north of 3,000 individual pieces of copy in the last 23 years. They include lots of sales letters and brochures, plus press releases, press ads and presentations, websites, emails, and banner ads. And the odd menu, speech, and poster. My first efforts weren't bad (well, OK, some of them were): the stuff I'm writing now earns my clients enough profits for them to keep coming back for more. I want to share with you some of the tricks of the trade that I've used over that period to keep my clients happy; I hope they'll work their magic for you, whether you're a freelance, agency, or in-house copywriter. Most are my own, some are borrowed, or adapted, from other copywriters.

A couple of paragraphs ago I used the word "selling." In many people's houses, though not ours, selling is a dirty word. It conjures up associations of foot-in-the-door brush salesmen, high-pressure selling, boiler rooms, and other equally unsavory activities and individuals. But the truth is, without selling, there'd be no markets. Without markets, there'd be no capitalism. Without capitalism, there'd be no democracy. And without democracy, there'd be no freedom. So as you can see, without selling, we'd all be in chains!

And let's scotch another myth about copywriting. We are not paid liars. I was once cornered at a party by a guy who actually *was* a salesman, for a confectionery manufacturer. When I told him what I did for a living, he said, "Oh right. A paid bullshitter." That, regrettably, is how many people think about advertising. I prefer David Ogilvy's take on truth in advertising: "Never write an advertisement which you wouldn't want your family to read. You wouldn't tell lies to your own wife. Don't tell them to mine."

Leaving aside this little bit of special pleading, even when I'm training marketeers and copywriters, many still don't see the connection between what they're doing and selling. Or don't want to see it. But it's worth reminding ourselves that we *are* salespeople. It sounds good to tell your friends you're a copywriter. You imagine they see you as some kind of über-wordsmith, composing witty and creative advertising copy on a laptop while swinging to and fro in your Scandinavian-designed office chair listening to cool music on your iPod. Yeah, right. When I tell other parents I meet in my boys' school playground that I'm a copywriter the usual reaction is either, "OK, what's that?" or "That's interesting because I've got an idea I want to copyright." Hmm. Now I say, "I help companies sell more by writing about their products. You know, for mailshots and websites." Then everybody gets it. So, you're in sales. I am too. The question is, are you any good?

Well, you buy books on copywriting. That means you are very good already or you intend to become very good. It's only the ignorant, the uninterested, and the unambitious who don't read books that could help them get on professionally. So what about this one? I'm guessing it's not the first book on copywriting you've read or even bought. And it's a very different kind of book to the majority out there on Amazon and the shelves of your local bookstore.

For a start, you don't need to read it all the way through. The 100 ideas presented here all stand alone. You could read one printed on a trackside poster at a rail station and it would do its job. Nor do you have to read the ideas in sequence. This book, and the series of which it forms a part, is expressly designed for you to dip in and out. Some of the ideas have explicit titles you could flick to to solve a particular problem; Idea 5, for example, shows you how to handle objections in your headline. Others are more elliptically titled, such as Idea 76, Act like a magpie.

What it won't do is teach you about the theory of copywriting. Or how to write specific *kinds* of copy, emails for example, or press ads. Nor will it teach you how to become a freelance copywriter. What it will do, I hope, is prime your imagination with a set of ideas you could try out in your own copy to improve it and help you sell more stuff.

A final note: throughout the book I use the words "reader" and "prospect" more or less interchangeably. "Reader" because this is about writing, and "prospect" because it's also about selling.

The ideas

Ideas are the lifeblood of great copy. Here are 100 of mine you can transfuse into your own writing. Not all are purely about copywriting: as well as running my own business I have often been asked to advise clients, so my insights into the selling process go far wider than the copy you write for your website or sales letter.

Most of the ideas draw on copy I have written for hundreds of clients since I started my agency, Sunfish, in 1996. Sometimes I have quoted directly from it, other ideas use the copy as a springboard for a more general discussion of a particular technique. In each case I have tried to give you a sense not just of what works, but why it works and how you could use it yourself. I like telling stories too, which is why so many include situations and dialog from jobs I've worked on. And although, like most independent and freelance copywriters, I'll sell anything, or almost anything, I specialize in subscriptions copywriting, which means a fair few examples are drawn from the publishing industry. These ideas, though, have a much wider application, especially if you work on products with the potential for repeat purchase of any kind, not just subscriptions.

Some of the ideas talk specifically about web copywriting. But you can apply all of them to almost any channel. People do not react differently to copy just because they're reading it on a screen rather than a piece of paper. They may be more ready to stop reading, however, and that calls for an even more relentless focus on the first of the themes I outline next.

Three themes that unite the 100 ideas in the book

Your reader matters most. When you set out to write copy for a new campaign, you, your manager, or your client may want to include all sorts of "messages" about your product. But readers don't care about messages. They care about one thing: themselves. Or, in less blunt but more circular terms, they care about the things they care about. Which, invariably, do not include whatever you're pitching. So if you're going to interest them in what you're selling, you have to explain—and prove—how it will make their life easier or better in some way.

Readers are human beings. And, as such, are prone to all the wonderful, frustrating, natural emotions that make us what we are. They are lazy sometimes, greedy, ambitious, envious even; but also caring, kind, passionate, and humane. Learn to speak to them as people, as you would if you met them in a bar. Your language should be the sort of language your readers use themselves.

Copywriting is a craft skill not an art form. Yes, it helps if you have a gift for language but even without that gift, you can make a good living as a copywriter, or make millions for your employer, if you practice. Study good copywriting, figure out why it works, and copy it. Yes, copy it. Not word for word (except as an academic exercise) but copy its structure, style, and any devices you think would work well for your product. And forget about creativity. Concentrate on results instead.

Andy Maslen

IT'S NOT ABOUT YOU (OR IS IT?)

REMEMBER THAT CLASSIC scene in the 1976 movie *Taxi Driver*? As Travis Bickle, the somewhat unhinged taxi driver of the title, Robert De Niro stares at himself in the mirror of his apartment, brandishing a large-caliber handgun and uttering his famous speech that begins, "You talkin' to me . . . ?"

The problem with a lot of copy is that it isn't "talkin' to me." If anything it's talkin' *at* me. That's a big difference because the center of the universe in that kind of copy is the writer. But who cares about the writer? Certainly not the reader.

The idea

From Magnet, a kitchen company

The way to ensure your reader feels you are talking to them is to use one simple little word, over and over. That word is "you." So in answer to the question that heads this idea, it *is* about you, if by you we mean the reader not the writer.

Here's a great press ad for Magnet that begins by talking to the reader and never lets up . . .

> It's only by getting to know you, your wants, needs, and desires that Magnet can create kitchens that are as individual as you are.

In 87 words of body copy, "you" or "your" appears eight times. There are just three references to Magnet. In fact that's just about the perfect ratio of reader:writer at 2.7:1.

Why this works is because from the reader's perspective, the copy is all about them: their concerns, their motivations, their problems. It's like talking to someone at a party who asks you lots of questions about yourself. We always warm to people like that because they give us a chance to talk about ourselves.

Conversely, if you keep using "I" and "we," your copy starts to sound remote and boring. After all, they didn't *ask* you to write a mailshot or email to them, so you'd better make it relevant to them. They may have stopped turning the page or clicking away because your headline was compelling enough to make them want to know more. But the moment you start banging on about yourself, you lose them.

In practice

- When you're writing copy, try to imagine a single reader sitting in front of you. That's who you're writing to. Not your "audience," your "target market," or your "visitors." Just this one individual with whom you hope to establish a relationship that will lead to a sale.

- Aim for two to three "you"s to every "I." This magic ratio guarantees that your copy will be more about your reader than it is about you. And that will keep them interested.

2 REMEMBER, YOU'RE SELLING

Perhaps because a lot of people who write copy do it because they love words, they can sometimes forget why they're writing in the first place. Here are a few things we're *not* doing. Impressing our reader with the depth of our vocabulary. Making them laugh. Producing literary fiction (or any other kind for that matter). Writing prose poems. Now here's the thing we *are* doing. Ready?

Selling.

Remember, we're only writing copy because visiting each of our prospects personally is beyond our resources. And if we were able to do that, we'd spend our time selling, not passing the time with beautiful but pointless conversation.

What does selling mean? OK, without writing another book, how about this: selling means identifying who's in the market for your products and services, identifying why they might want it, why they might be holding back, persuading them of the value, then closing the deal.

The idea

From Waitrose Wine Direct, a supermarket's mail-order wine offering

When you're writing copy about something fun, or entertaining or enjoyable—such as wine—there's a real temptation to go off on an extended bit of color copy. You know, you just let your mind go, pour a glass of the product (for research purposes, naturally) and before you know it you've written three or four hundred words of fancy copy, painting a picture of Tuscan picnics, Ancien Régime Châteaux in the Loire Valley, or wine tours around the Napa Valley. Trouble is, you've left your reader cold and forgotten to sell them anything. Waitrose Wine Direct do it differently. In a mailer I received at home, the letter begins with some juicy lines to get me in the mood . . .

> As I am writing this the sun is finally shining, the temperature is rising and all I want to do is to be outside and enjoy a crisp white on the hammock or perhaps a lightly chilled red as the barbecue heats up.

So far, so good. Though I worry about drinking wine in a hammock. But before it all gets a bit too "Year in Tuscany," we get smacked between the eyes with the first of many offers . . .

> With its crisp and fresh style, Sauvignon Blanc is a great summer white and the Summer Sauvignon Blanc mixed case on page four is not only great value with £29 off but also a fantastic crowd pleaser.

Ah. Good old-fashioned selling. Get the product in front of the prospect. Describe it. Make the offer sound unmissable. And show them how they can get kudos from their friends for serving it.

In practice

- Imagine you are face to face with your customer. Now write a script for what you'd say. You can start off softly, but you're going to want to come to the point fairly quickly before they start checking their watch.

- It's fine to write copy that creates a receptive mood for buying. Just make sure it doesn't become an end in itself.

HEADLINE IDEA—YOUR READER IS SELFISH

You CAN'T BE a copywriter without also being a student of human nature. Oh, OK, you can . . . *If* you're content to churn out lines like "As a valued customer, I'm delighted to tell you we've totally redesigned our website." But on the assumption this doesn't apply to *you*, it means you are curious about what makes people tick. And by now you should have discovered that people are basically selfish.

That just means they want to know why they should do whatever you're asking them to. The old "What's in it for me?" question. And so, in your headlines, you could do a lot worse than to address their self-interest directly.

The idea

From John Caples, legendary copywriter

When you're selling, it pays to reach out to your reader's motivations. But a lot of copywriters start off by trying to *make* people feel motivated, maybe by explaining a problem or creating anxiety about a bad situation. Here's a newsflash: you can't make people feel motivation. All you can do is identify what they're already motivated by and address that issue.

When you're writing a headline, why not assume that there's a readymade audience for your pitch out there and all you have to do is call to them by using their motivation? Their self-interest, in other words.

John Caples, one of the all-time-great copywriters and author of *Tested Advertising Methods*, once wrote an ad for the Phoenix Mutual Life Insurance Company. The headline read:

To Men Who Want to Quit Work Someday.

Picture the ad with that line under a photo of a guy of retirement age fishing from his boat and looking directly out at you with a big smile on his face. The headline—in concert with the photo—is saying, in effect, "If you want a worry-free retirement where you can indulge your hobbies without fretting over money, read on." And reading on is all the headline needs to achieve. After that it's up to the body copy to take the pass and run with the ball all the way to the touchdown.

Your reader is interested in a lot of different things—all related to their own well-being. A short and definitely non-exclusive list could include social status, more money, more free time, good health, security for their family, lower taxes, self-esteem, a new car every two years, being popular, or paying off the mortgage. Find a way to zero in on the right motivation in your headline and you've achieved the dream—you've stopped your reader from ignoring your message.

In practice

- If you were trying to stop your reader boarding a train by calling out to them, what would you shout? That's the first draft of your headline.

- Think of all the ways your reader would benefit from what you're selling. Then rank them in order of power and choose number one for your headline.

4 THE CALL TO ACTION

Take a random group of 1,000 sales executives and ask them to arrange themselves in a very long line, according to how much commission they made last year, big hitters on the right, Willy Lomans on the left. After a bit of a wait (OK, you could finish reading this book), they're done.

I guarantee that among the skills shared by the big hitters is this one. They are all great closers. And that means they know how to ask for the order. Which we, as copywriters, need to be great at too. It's called "the call to action."

The idea

From City Equities Limited, a licensed equities dealer

The call to action (CTA) is usually the line or paragraph at the end of an email, brochure, or letter inviting the reader to respond. Most often, the desired response is an order of some kind. But it might be signing up to an email newsletter, reserving a place on a free seminar, or even just confirming receipt.

Logically, the CTA goes at the end. That's where the selling finishes and the closing starts. Or does it? You could have a CTA in the headline. Or you could pepper your copy with CTAs after each new benefit or section. After all, you never know how soon your reader will have been convinced by your crystalline prose.

City Equities say, "When you reply to my letter, one of our dealers will telephone you to learn more about your investment requirements."

I'd call this an assumptive close. We're telling the reader what will happen *when* they respond. Not if.

Just as the CTA seems to go last, it often gets written last. But maybe that's not such a good idea. After all, you're tired . . . and elated . . . the letter is almost finished. You can go home. Just as soon as that pesky call to action is done. So you dash off an "order now," save and close, and you're clear.

But this is the whole point of the letter (or ad, flyer, or web page). This is where it all comes down to a "yes" or "no" from your reader. So it needs the most effort, creativity, and precision to get it right.

In practice

- Write your CTA first. Apart from anything else, it will help you focus on your goal, whether that's new orders, sales leads, or sign-ups to an e-zine.

- You can use a CTA to get people to do anything, even turn the page on a two-page letter.

ANOTHER HEADLINE IDEA—OBJECTION HANDLING

THE TROUBLE WITH headlines promising benefits is people are so darned cynical these days. You can't blame them though. Decades of being subjected to spurious sales claims and rubbish attempts at wordplay by generations of hacks have left them about as trusting as turkeys at Christmas.

For every benefit there's a reader saying, "Well, you would say that, but what if . . . ?" And it's the "what if?" question that lies behind the "What's in it for me?" question, whispering poison into the reader's ear. "Oh sure," it says. "They *say* you'll lose weight. But you'll probably have to eat wood shavings, or stewed grass for a month. Turn the page."

The idea

From a cellphone manufacturer

This manufacturer is advertising a cool bit of software that lets workers pick up their emails on their cellphones without incurring more costs, a big objection from the finance directors who have to sign off on this type of corporate expenditure. They do this with a headline that reads something like this:

Now: email on-the-go without hidden charges.

Whatever you're selling, you have to overcome your prospect's reservations, objections, and "what ifs" before you make the sale. And doing it in the headline is pretty clever. So a useful little technique when you're writing a headline is to think about the reader's objections, as well as their motivations. In other words, what's *stopping* them reading on, rather than what would *make* them read on.

Suppose you were selling a weight-loss plan to an affluent group of consumers you knew liked their first growth Bordeaux. An OK headline would be:

> Lose weight now

But the what-ifster would be whispering, "You don't really believe that do you? You know you'll have to give up drinking." So how about:

> How Parisian women are losing 7lb in a fortnight without giving up their vin rouge

It's longer, sure: 15 words as opposed to three. But it's stronger because it overcomes the objection. There's also a compelling narrative that helps the reader identify with the copy. It's specific. It tells the reader how much weight she'll shed and in what time. And "Parisian women" conjures up a picture of chic, svelte ladies in smart clothes—an aspirational image for the reader.

In practice

- Remember that your reader is likely to be skeptical at best and cynical at worst about claims made by advertising copy. So try to allay their fears with a subtle or bold answer to the "what if?" question.

- Look at your own headlines. Assuming you've stuffed them full of benefits, could they work even harder if you found a way to address an objection?

6 BUSINESSPEOPLE LOVE OFFERS TOO

In BUSINESS-TO-consumer promotions, everyone uses offers. I'm sure you're familiar with the kind of thing I'm talking about: get a free calendar, save £10, win a holiday. But in business-to-business, some marketeers are a little wary. "Our customers are too sophisticated; they'll see what we're trying to do" is a common reason given for not running an offer.

Well, it's true that businesspeople are clever and complex creatures, but they also love an offer. After all, businesspeople are consumers, too, and they respond to offers addressed to them at home, don't they?

The idea

From an international research consultancy

One of the best offers I ever ran for a client was a pocket calculator that we bought in for £3 as an incentive on a £550 reference book. We had librarians falling over themselves to place their orders and saw a big uplift in response. For a cheap calculator. These people must have owned at least two calculators each already. But it was free. (And let's remember that "free" is one of the best words any copywriter has at his or her fingertips.) If you're not already using offers to lift response on your mailings, now would be an excellent time to start testing. Here are a few things to remember:

Always limit your offer. Either by time, which is probably the most common way, or by quantity. To limit by time, you could say, "Reply by October 31st and you'll save 10%." Or "Remember, you must reply by October 31st to claim your free pen." To limit by quantity, you could try "The first 100 people to reply will each get a free clock." Or "Reply today. If you're one of the lucky 50, you'll be spending a day at a luxury health spa."

Always repeat your offer. In a mailpack you've got the outer, the letter, and the brochure and you may also have a reply envelope. These are all opportunities to reinforce the message that they could get FREE STUFF for replying. But couch the offer in varying language so you don't simply repeat yourself.

Consider putting your offer in your main headline. Lots of very successful promotions lead on the offer; for example, a headline might say "Get £10 of dry cleaning vouchers when you send us your first suit." Test your offers. Do people respond better to the offer of free stuff when they order at full price, or do they like the idea of a discount?

Whatever you decide to do, bear in mind that *everyone* likes getting a good deal and everyone wants something for nothing.

In practice

- Make the offer fit the action required. Offering a gift worth £100 for a buying decision valued at £50 looks odd. Your respondent is likely to think "What's the catch?"

- If you're offering a saving on the full price, try to express it as both a percentage saving and a cash amount: different things appeal to different people.

WRITE AS YOU SPEAK

I WAS SITTING in the cinema recently, waiting for the movie to start. After the ads and the trailers, we were treated to this screen announcement: "The management regrets the necessity of informing patrons that the safety of personal valuables cannot be guaranteed and they should not be placed where they cannot be seen."

A bemused, then amused, murmur went around as we worked out what it meant: "Keep your bags safe: don't put them on the floor."

That started me thinking about the way we dress up perfectly simple messages in stifling layers of unnecessary language. It's almost as if we're ashamed to let our words out of doors unadorned.

The idea

From Hox Brasserie, a Salisbury restaurant

This upmarket Indian restaurant in Salisbury is a cut above the typical neighborhood "curry house." The owner, Atiqul Hoque, wanted to create a very personal-sounding menu with a letter from him at the very beginning. Here it is, in full:

Dear Customer, The Spanish say, "My house is your house." I'd like to say to you, "My restaurant is your restaurant."

I want you to feel like a regular here, even if it's your first visit. And if you're coming back, I hope it's because we delighted you last time with our friendly approach (and of course, our authentic, original—and delicious—food).

Bringing wonderful Indian food to people from Salisbury and the surrounding area is my passion, and I'd love you to share it. Not just by coming here to eat, but by offering your suggestions for new dishes. We'll take your ideas seriously—that's a promise.

Whether you are looking for dinner for two, a family lunch, a wedding celebration, or even a business function, you'll find we have the space, the service, and the desire to make your occasion a very special occasion indeed.

I came to Salisbury over ten years ago. I always dreamt of opening a restaurant where my customers could come with their friends, families, and colleagues to sit down and enjoy some truly inspirational Indian cooking. That dream has come true. Welcome to Hox Brasserie.

Remember that copy is simply a substitute (and a poor one at that) for a conversation you ought to be having with individual customers.

In practice

- Start by writing down what you'd say to someone if you were talking to them. It won't be perfect, but it will be a good start, couched in the kind of natural language that people use themselves every day.

- Once you have the first draft in Plain English you can look for errors of grammar, or punctuation, or phrasing; you won't have to worry that you sound like a Victorian civil servant.

8 WISH YOU WERE HERE

HAVE YOU EVER got a postcard in your morning's post and *not* read it? Me neither. There's something compelling about that small, stiff piece of card that says "Read me." So why not consider putting that factor to work for you in your marketing campaigns?

Postcards have a number of advantages over traditional mailpacks. They're cheaper, there's no need for an envelope, they have instant visual appeal, they only need one hand to read, they have a "fun factor," and they look less daunting. As a series, you can also use them to communicate a complex idea in stages, drip-feeding information to your target without overtaxing them.

The idea

From a computer services company

I once wrote an eight-card series for this client, promoting a new IT maintenance contract. The idea was to stimulate awareness among corporate IT managers and build their database.

We announced on the first card that there would be a quiz on the final one with a prize of a day's tank driving. The hook was that the questions would relate to the information provided on the first seven cards—a big incentive to look out for them and keep reading. They achieved maximum exposure for minimum outlay and gained lots of new names for their database, too.

Because you don't need an envelope, you can also throw away the rule book about acceptable sizes. Yes, you can have an A5 or an A6 postcard. But why not try a half-page A4 vertical format? Or a 100mm square? Or a circle? There are cost considerations, as always, but talking to your printer (or designer) will help you balance creativity against paper wastage.

Whatever you do with it, your postcard—mono, two-color, or full color—adds another component to your marketing campaigns, increases your flexibility, and gives your customers/prospects a break from the run of mailshots they're used to.

In practice

- Once you've printed your postcard, you can use it different ways. As a self-mailer, an insert, a flyer, an exhibition giveaway, or a component of your press kit.

- Why not investigate digital printing for your postcard? You can incorporate your target's name (and any other variable data you like) into the design. In color.

ON THE WEB, IT'S (EVEN MORE) PERSONAL

ATTEND AN INTERNET marketing conference these days and there is a very good chance you will hear a presentation on writing for the web. But what the guru advises turns out not to be so very different from what the greats of advertising and direct marketing copywriting have been saying for the last 100 years or so.

The guru will take as his (or, less frequently, her) whipping boy a piece of cloddy, hubristic, advertising copy—from a corporate brochure, perhaps. "This," they intone, "just won't wash on the web." Well, I'm sorry, but it didn't wash in print either. It's just that it was quite hard to tell.

The idea

From a social club for upmarket sport fans

A while ago now, I wrote some web copy for a company bringing together sporty/horsey types. We wanted to capture the energy of the sports themselves and present the benefits of the club through copy that sounded like the company's founder was talking directly to the site visitor.

Here are a couple of paragraphs:

> Watching your horse come from behind to win by a head. Seeing the match turn on a last-minute drop-goal. Discussing form with leading jockeys and trainers. There are many ways to set your pulse racing. And joining Racing Pulses gives you privileged access to them all.

As a Racing Pulses member, you're in good—no, make that great—company. Our members are single, sociable and sporting. Mostly 25 and over, they come from the professions, from farming, from town and country. London lawyers, Yorkshire farmers, West Country entrepreneurs, and racing media professionals: you'll meet them all.

So, how do we achieve that all-important personal tone of voice? It turns out that good web copy is much the same as good direct marketing copy. Or, for that matter, good essays, love letters, or notes for the milkman. Let me give you a couple of simple rules that help . . .

In practice

- Write in a conversational, even chatty style. Use Plain English and don't be afraid to sound more informal than you might in print.

- Never, ever write "some of you" on a web page (or in an email). Yes, more than one person will visit the page. More than one might even be reading it at the same time. *But not as far as they're concerned.*

GRAMMAR DOESN'T MATTER . . . OR DOES IT?

CONVERSATION AROUND YOUR dinner party table flagging? At least one guest over 30? Start a fight by suggesting that grammar doesn't matter in advertising. (Or, if you want to be cleaning red wine sauce off your ceiling for weeks, that it doesn't matter anywhere at all.)

Does it matter whether national brand advertising is grammatically correct? David Ogilvy declared he didn't know the rules of grammar. Read his ads and you can see that he did. You can write copy that is hard-hitting, persuasive, even entertaining *and* also avoid trashing the English language. But maybe there's something that matters even more than correct English, something to do with the fundamental truths about your product. Like is it any good? Do enough people want to pay for it? And, ultimately, will your revenues from selling it outweigh your costs in producing and promoting it?

The idea

From a credit card company (now defunct)

Driving home from London one weekend, we passed a poster for a particularly fashionable credit card brand. In their infinite wisdom, the credit card company, or their advertising agency, managed to create a headline of such stunning illiteracy that my five-year-old picked it up.

Maybe the "creatives" put their heads together and tossed around two versions of the same headline—good and bad grammar—before deciding the bad version was more populist or some other crappy justification. Maybe they just didn't know the difference. Either way, it provided more ammunition for the "all advertising is rubbish" brigade. *However* . . . that's not my point.

Although the self-proclaimed "creative community" seemed to be having a collective you-know-what over this "brilliant viral campaign," the card itself was already in deep doo-doo, commercially. The brand owners had just written off almost half a billion dollars of losses and a quick trawl through a few personal finance chatboards or money comparison sites revealed the awful truth.

No doubt the marketing department and their agencies were hoping for many awards and accompanying champagne dinners. No doubt they got them. But did all the brouhaha about the advertising turn around the fortunes of the brand? Well, as it now no longer exists, I guess that would be a "no."

In practice

- Provided you can write simple sentences in Plain English, grammar shouldn't be an issue for your copywriting. Concentrate on expressing your concept clearly and all should be well.

- No amount of good grammar will save a toxic brand, so make sure the product is solid before worrying about the subjunctive.

WHAT NOT TO PUT ON YOUR ORDER FORM

WHENEVER I GET a mailshot in the post, or look at a direct response ad in the paper, I always read the order form first. It's become a little game . . . seeing whether they've gone for the easy option or been creative. And specifically, I look at the headline.

I get a point every time I see the words "Order form." So far I have roughly 85 million points. Why, after getting all the way through the sales process to the close, do these copywriters shrug their shoulders and start *labelling* things? There has to be something more compelling to write than "Order form" doesn't there?

The idea

From order forms labeled "Order form"

When you're writing a direct response ad or mailshot, I'm willing to bet you write the order form last. We all tend to think linearly about copywriting, starting from the outside in. So, outer, letter, brochure, response device. Which means by the time we get around to the order form itself, we're feeling just a couple of steps away from the finish line.

The result is often recourse to the boilerplate bin. Need a headline? "Order form" should do it. After all, it *is* an order form. But that's precisely my point. There are plenty of clues to tip off even the doziest reader that this is, indeed, the order form. Credit card symbols, lines for entering their personal details, return address, direct debit mandate, and so on.

And it's not as if we resort to labeling any other parts of the pack. The outer envelope, for example, rarely carries the line "Outer envelope." And I'm fairly sure I've never seen a sales letter with "Top flap" written above the body copy.

If you were selling face to face, and the customer had just agreed to buy from you, would you say, "Great! Can I just get you to fill in this form?" No! You'd say, "Great! Let's just get this paperwork done and I can give you your free steak knives." In other words, turn the close into another pleasurable part of the process, not form-filling.

There are lots of things you could write that would keep the smile on the customer's face long enough for you to close the sale. Recap the main benefit, for example. Or remind them of what they'll lose if they don't buy.

In practice

- Write your order form first. That way you come to it fresh.

- Treat the order form as an ad in its own right. Spend some time thinking of a headline that encourages the reader to make the purchase. "Order now" is far, far better than "Order form."

SUBJECT LINES

Do YOU USE emails as part of your promotional mix? If you do, I bet you spend a long time working on the message: lots of nice short sentences (balanced with longer ones, of course); plenty of benefits; calls to action top and bottom; hot buttons. But let me ask you a question . . .

How much time do you spend on the subject line? This is the critical part of the package; yet it's often overlooked. It can galvanize your reader into opening the email or it can have them stabbing the Trash button.

The idea

From a company promoting car care products via email

A while back, I had a classic car: a beautiful, two-tone silver/burgundy 1973 Rover V8 Coupé. I probably spent more time polishing it than driving it. (Maybe because it always seemed to be breaking down.) Classic car nuts love lavishing TLC on their vehicles so they're a natural market for any kind of product that promises a superior shine. Here's the subject line from an American company that makes a range of car (and boat) care products:

Andy, Give Your Cherished Classic a Showroom Shine in Minutes!

We've got my first name (which they'd captured online). People tend to scan their inbox downwards, not left to right like normal reading. So your hot words need to be upfront where they'll get picked up. But right after the name—whammo!—the benefit. In fact it's two benefits. First you can get that wet-look shine that makes you want to park your car where you—and others—can see it. Second you can do it quickly. That sounds like big results for basically no work. (Because everybody's lazy, right?)

If you've come from a direct mail background, you should be a natural. The subject line is your outer envelope. But just look at the height of the bar you have to clear. You've got no color, no paper, no windows showing glimpses of the pack inside, no logo—just a few characters.

And I mean a few. Some years ago now, Anne Holland of MarketingSherpa was recommending 40. In fact with growing numbers of readers opening emails on their BlackBerry, I'd say even 40 characters was pushing it. As inboxes get more and more crowded, people are actively looking for reasons not to open emails of any kind, let alone promotional ones. So the secret is to give them a reason to click. And that means giving them the benefit.

In practice

- Put the good stuff upfront, where people can see it. You can't guarantee your reader will go right to the end of your subject line before deciding whether to open or not.

- Write your message first, then you've got a platform to create a winning subject line.

AVOID CLICHÉS (LIKE THE PLAGUE)

STEALING IDEAS IS a great idea. If they're good ones. But stealing rotten ideas, just because you've seen them elsewhere, is just plain dim. Clichés abound in copywriting and they come in many guises, from the everyday to the industry-specific, from corporate jargon to marketing-speak.

They might make the writer feel good about themselves but they do little for the reader except to generate a sense of déjà vu. The big problem is that clichés encourage the reader to assume *all* your copy is just a boring retread of ideas and phrases they've all heard a thousand times already.

The idea

From too many advertisers to mention individually

As a valued client . . .

What's wrong with using this phrase to start an email or sales letter? After all, they *are* a valued client, so what could be more pleasant than telling them? Well, here's the thing. If you use a cliché to open a letter to your valued clients, the subtext is unambiguous:

> Dear Mr Sample, I hold your custom in such slight regard that rather than spend two minutes thinking of a new and personal way to address you, I used this rusty old cliché.

You know it's a cliché: you've seen it a million times. And if you have, so has your client. Why not start by saying:

Dear Mr Sample, I want to thank you for being a regular customer. So the next time you call to place an order, please call me on my direct line—020 555 1234—and I'll make sure we give you a 25% loyalty discount.

Or . . .

Dear Mr Sample, Your custom is important to us at Watkins Widgets of Wolverhampton. So, as a "thank you," please accept the enclosed voucher for a free trial pack of our new ExecutivePlus Non-slip Luminous Widgets.

See what I mean? It takes a little thought, and a little time, but your client ends up thinking that maybe, just maybe, you *do* actually care about him.

At the end of the day, you shouldn't touch clichés with a bargepole. Whichever way you look at it, they don't fly. They're dead in the water. They're . . . [*That's enough clichés—Ed.*] OK—the truth?

The world is saturated with marketing messages. Most of them are flat, poorly thought through, and amateurish in their execution. Think harder than the other guys, spend a little more time, effort, and money, and you can stand away from the herd as they stampede wildly for the cliff top.

In practice

- Set your cliché scanner to "high." If it sounds familiar and overworked to you, just imagine the impact (or lack of it) that it has on your reader.

- Whenever you find yourself using a cliché, rewrite it in Plain English. Customers will be more engaged with your copy and that means more sales.

14 KEEP IT SHORT

COPYWRITERS (MYSELF INCLUDED), direct marketing agencies, and clients have shown, over and over again, that long copy outpulls short. So why am I suggesting you keep it short? Well, this idea isn't so much about the overall length of your copy as its conciseness.

If you can make a point in eight words, don't use 15. If you can make your point in three words, why use eight? A willingness to be ruthless when editing your copy will tighten it up like a racing yacht's rigging, yielding every last drop of performance.

The idea

From Winston Churchill

I used this quote in my first book, *Write to Sell*, so my apologies if you've seen it before. But it bears repeating (and rereading) because of its amazing power.

Churchill wrote this telegram on August 10, 1942 to General Alexander, Commander in Chief in the Middle East:

> Your prime and main duty will be to take or destroy at the earliest opportunity the German-Italian army commanded by Field Marshal Rommel together with all its supplies and establishments in Egypt and Libya.

Wow! In just 35 words, he packed in an entire campaign, from target to objectives and timescale.

When you sit down to write your next piece of copy, remember this. You may be passionate about the product you're selling—either because you invented it, you're trading it, you manufacture it, or you supply it personally. But your reader probably isn't. Blathering on about it won't bring the sale any closer.

Make sure you use tight, muscular language where every word counts. Don't say it's "27 meters in length," say it's "27 meters long." Don't say, "We are located in the city of Birmingham." Say, "We're in Birmingham."

If you end up cutting your first draft by 30 percent, fine. You now have all that free space to write more benefits-laden copy. Or, you can decide you've said all you need to make the sale, and your reader has to do less work before making their buying decision.

In practice

- Don't worry about being concise when you're writing your first draft. Instead, concentrate on telling the reader a compelling story about your product and why they should buy it. Leave the editing until your second draft.

- Watch for empty adjectives, clichés, waffle, repetition, redundancy, and, in particular, writing that pleases you but leaves the reader cold.

SHINY, BRIGHT, EXCITING ADJECTIVES

A YOUNG GIRL was going into school to take her English exam. Her mother checked her uniform, made sure she had a pen that worked, then uttered this piece of advice: "Remember, dear: two adjectives to every noun and you'll be sure to pass."

It's a style of writing that many people cling to in later life, too. Even copywriters. But not the greats. You see, it turns out that larding your prose with adjectives achieves precisely the opposite effect to the one you are striving for.

The idea

From too many companies to name individually

Just as a diet high in fat furs up your arteries like old water pipes, so a profusion of adjectives clogs up your writing and makes it harder to get the meaning through. And let's be clear—we are always striving to communicate an idea. Clearly, vividly, and concisely. So why are adjectives so dangerous? Essentially, because all too often they allow the lazy writer to avoid the work of researching the subject and choosing the precise noun.

Lazy writers don't bother bringing their product or service to life; they leave all the hard work to the reader. Let's look at an example from the "super, smashing, great" school of adjectival overuse:

The conference will close with an exciting acrobatic display.

This writer has fallen back on our old pal, "exciting" as a substitute for thought. Let's suppose we've found out a bit more about the display.

The conference will close with a display of acrobatics, performed by five members of China's Olympic team. They will climb a 100ft pole before diving head first into a hogshead of real fire.

Notice that where we do use adjectives, they are telling the reader more about the thing they're describing, not merely puffing it. In other words, use adjectives to add information, not emphasis.

In practice

- If you want to tighten up a piece of copy, you could do worse than cut every adjective. Focus on choosing the precise noun, rather than qualifying vague or abstract ones with adjectives.

- And be particularly wary of emotional adjectives, like fabulous, important, exciting, fantastic. It's for your reader to feel these things, not for you to dictate them. Show them *why* something deserves these badges and let them pin them on.

16 IMAGINE . . .

ONE OF THE simplest techniques for getting your reader to engage with your copy is to ask them to use their imagination. And the simplest way to do this is to use the verb "imagine." Telling people to imagine something engages far more of their brain than simply writing about your product.

Instead, you give them license to daydream—a far more pleasurable activity than reading. Then all you have to do is create a place for them where that daydream leads, inexorably, to interest in whatever you're selling.

The idea

From dreamcarhire.com, a sports car hire firm

As a self-confessed petrolhead, I love everything to do with fast cars. And I guess like a lot of people, I'd love to tool around in a Ferrari for a day—or longer. But until that lottery win or inheritance from a mystery millionaire relative, it's going to have to stay as just a dream. Or is it? Because, of course, for every dream we in the West can conjure up, there's at least one outfit catering to its fulfillment. In the case of sports car hire, there are dozens, from membership clubs to straightforward hire companies.

Flicking through the back pages of *Top Gear* magazine, I came upon a really great ad for dreamcarhire.com. As an aside, it follows the ideal ad layout, as used by great copywriters from David Ogilvy and John Caples on down: picture, headline, body copy, call to action, logo.

We have a full-width photo of a glossy black Ferrari F430, landscape blurred behind it. But it's the headline that really brings you up short and lets the ad do its work:

Imagine yourself behind the wheel of a supercar

It's a powerful little eight-word phrase, supercharged by the word "imagine." Why? Because that's precisely what the reader is doing anyway. So the copywriter has tapped directly into the motivation of the reader. They could have just written . . .

You could be driving this supercar

But then we're left feeling, "Yeah right, but only for a day." It's a downer.

Or

Driving a supercar needn't cost the earth

But now we're focused on cost, even as the copywriter strives to sell the benefits of hiring. But the "imagine" headline takes us beyond the sell, beyond the close, into the territory the copywriter wants us to inhabit: *life with the product.*

In practice

- Start by thinking about how the world would look to your reader if they did the thing you wanted them to. Create a quick pencil portrait of this scene.

- Write some copy starting with the phrase "Imagine a world in which you . . ." Now complete it with the details of your pen portrait. New paragraph: "It's all possible when you . . ."

17 PARTING IS SUCH SWEET SORROW (ACTUALLY, IT'S JUST SORROW)

MAGAZINE, JOURNAL, AND newsletter publishers know that existing subscribers are far more profitable than new acquisitions. That's why they spend so much time, money, and effort trying to hold onto them.

Think of your customers as subscribers and you can use many of the techniques publishers use. One of the most common is the renewal series. This is a set of letters, emails, and other communications mailed to subscribers as their subscription comes up for renewal.

If you're marketing any kind of service where people sign up for a fixed period, you can use a renewal series.

The idea

From William Reed Business Media, a business information company

I've written a lot of marketing copy for *The Grocer*, William Reed's flagship food and drink magazine. Recently, they asked me to update their renewal series.

Here are five techniques I used in writing the various letters and emails.

1. Remind them of all the things they're about to stop getting. Using a phrase like "Extend your subscription (or membership) and you will still enjoy all this . . ." is a great way to start.

2. Suggest that they will be missing out on things other people will still be getting. Nobody likes to feel left out and if you play, subtly, on this fear, you can make people feel that they ought to renew.

3. Make it easy for them to renew. Don't stick complicated forms in front of your subscribers/members. Make it as simple as possible for them to renew and don't confuse them with too many options.

4. Use "extend" instead of "renew." Extend carries the sense of a continuing relationship, rather than one that comes to an end and has to be restarted each year. Really, we're only interested in how long they're going to renew for, rather than whether they're going to renew at all. In other words, our old friend the assumptive close.

5. Make an offer for early renewal and explain that there won't be any further better offers. You could use a phrase like "this is our best offer for existing subscribers." People will sometimes hold off on the renewal because they're convinced a better offer is just around the corner. You can push them off the fence by stating explicitly that this is the lowest price they're going to get.

In practice

- Write a plan for the timings, appeal, offer, tone of voice, and call to action for your renewal series.

- Include at least one letter using a regretful tone of voice. Explain that, although you personally would like nothing better than to continue having them as a subscriber, unless you receive their order it really will have to be goodbye.

18 LONG COPY AND WHY IT WORKS

It's FUNNY. EVEN people at the self-proclaimed "cutting edge" of copywriting—the web—turn out to be as fond of myths as their Stone Age (i.e., print) cousins. Here's one of my favorites: "Long copy doesn't work." This is usually uttered as an axiom so plainly true that no evidence is adduced to support it.

Truth is, we will keep reading. *If* we're reading something that interests us. Something that connects with a deep-seated need. Something that promises to bring our dreams a little closer. (Or actually within a hand's grasp.) The medium and the number of words are irrelevant.

The idea

From an audio system manufacturer

Unless you never read newspapers or magazines, you will have come across an ad for one of this high-end manufacturer's audio systems. From home cinema to CD and digital radio systems, they have a distinctive look and a niche in the market. And they always use long-copy ads.

Here are seven things we can see them doing to make their reader's life a little easier as they read the ads.

1. Short paragraphs.

2. Opening with a direct appeal to the reader's self-interest.

3. Plenty of bullet points and cross-heads to break up the page.

4. Press cuttings.

5. Talking directly to the reader: using "you" in other words (see Idea 1).

6. Lots of specifics.

7. Lots of benefits.

But maybe it's more complicated than saying, "long copy *does* work." Maybe it depends on what you're trying to achieve. Well, duh! If you're trying to get people to *do* something, like, oh I don't know, actually *buy* from you, there's a slim chance that they might want to know more about your product.

Obviously it depends what market you're in. If you're selling high-ticket management courses, you're going to need to say more than if you're selling garden bird feeders. Remember this, though. One of the main obstacles to people buying from you is *fear*. How are you going to allay their fears? Simple. You have to reassure them that it's safe to buy from you. And believe it or not, the more you say, the more reassured they feel.

In practice

- Don't worry about the length of your copy. The only people who will buy from you are people who are interested in what you're selling *already*. It stands to reason that they will want to know as much as possible about your product.

- Although your copy should say everything it needs to, keep individual copy elements brief. Short words, short sentences, short paragraphs all help your reader swallow your copy without getting indigestion.

DOES YOUR SERVICE LIVE UP TO THE COPY PROMISE?

A FEW YEARS ago, just after we moved in to our new house, I decided to buy a new lawnmower. A proper one. With an engine. Having identified the brand and spec I wanted, I pitched up at the local dealership looking for some advice and confirmation that my decision was the right one.

Presented with buying signals so clear even a mole could spot them, the salesperson palmed me off with a couple of brochures and pretty much showed me the door. Ho hum. Off I went to the net and found Classic Lawns. Not only was the copy inviting, clear, and, by the by, optimized for search engines, but it turned out to represent, accurately, what would happen if I placed an order.

The idea

From Classic Lawns, an online garden machinery retailer

Classic Lawns has a great website: easy to use and stuffed with testimonials and other proof of their commitment to customer service. And the following copy:

> Our Promise To You:
> We offer expert and professional advice
> Fast efficient delivery, often next working day
> We offer excellent after-care service.

But the really wonderful thing is that, two days after entering my credit card details, my shiny new mower arrived.

If you're running an e-commerce business, all the glitzy animation and slick web copy in the world won't work for you if your back-end is shaky. I contrast my experience of Classic Lawns with another gardening website that, somewhat grudgingly, promised delivery of items far smaller than a lawnmower in 14 days. Fourteen! In that time I could have walked to my local garden center and back and still had time left over to re-roof the shed.

And collect testimonials. If your business is as good as your website claims it is, your customers will send you letters and emails of appreciation without being asked. If it isn't, no matter. Go out and solicit them. On the web, you have to reassure people constantly that it's safe to do business with you. Real words from real customers are one of the most effective ways of doing this.

(I'd also like to praise Classic Lawns for selling lawnmowers, not "lawn solutions.")

In practice

● If you *give* great service, you don't need to witter on about your "passionate commitment to excellent customer service." This is a simple point often lost on large businesses with "dedicated" customer service departments.

● If you haven't done so recently, order something yourself from your own website and see what happens. Give your site a frustration rating and multiply that by the number of people ordering, or trying to, every week. Happy?

DO YOU DISSOLVE YOUR WORRIES IN A SOLUTION?

I WAS TAKING my children to school this morning and we saw a lovely big truck, on the side of which was emblazoned a picture of a window frame and the immortal line "joinery solutions." Son Number Two tugged on my hand and said, "Daddy, why doesn't he just say 'Handmade hardwood window frames'?" (My son is very advanced for his age.)

"Perhaps," I said, "he's worried that if he says that, people won't take him seriously." "Yes, Daddy," he said. "But now they don't know what makes him special." "Well then," I continued, a little nonplussed at this cross-examination, "maybe he thinks 'joinery solutions' is a modern thing to say." "But that's what everyone says now, Daddy. Thank goodness at school we have milk in the morning, not 'liquid dairy solutions.'"

The idea

From just about everyone

In just one week I have seen the following:

- "Delivering solutions globally."

- "Drinking water solutions."

- "Image solutions."

- "Customer relationship management solutions."

And best of all, by some considerable margin, in an advert for the lingerie section of a local department store:

- "Bra solutions."

This is what's known in the copywriting business as me-too-itis. The funny thing is, nobody who actually *buys* any of this stuff actually gives an expletive solution for "solution." Householders who want new wooden window frames generally call them just that. And, having checked with a couple of my female acquaintances, I can confidently assert that women go shopping for a new bra—not a new bra solution.

So what's going on? I suspect it has something to do with bored marketing executives wishing their products were more "exciting" and trying to jazz them up by hitching them to the s-word. Either that or imagining their customers will somehow feel cheated at being offered just a spade instead of an "excavation solution." This is just laziness. If you don't think "spade" is sufficient to sell spades, then do your research and be creative. Truly creative. Call it an "old-style, drop-forged spade with ash haft and non-blister grip." More people will buy it and you'll make more money.

In practice

- Of course you want your products to get customers salivating. But that means thinking about what they're *really* looking for, rather than just copying somebody else's lame copywriting idea.

- And yes, of course they want a solution to a problem of some kind, but what they *don't* want—or ever think of asking for—is a blah blah blah solution. Avoid.

CUSTOMERS OR CANNON FODDER?

CUSTOMERS ARE HARD enough to come by, heaven knows, without their leaving you as soon as they have what they want. No. What we need—all of us in business—is lifelong customers. People who love our products and way of doing business so much that they'll always come to us.

For that to happen, you need to build a relationship with them that transcends the mere exchange of goods for money. So what do you do to make your customers feel valued? How do you let them know that you care about them?

The idea

From Nationwide, a British building society

I have been e-banking with a particular building society for a few years now. I log onto my personal home page and see details of my account. When we moved house, we took out our new mortgage with the same company. Lo and behold, the next time I logged onto my home page, our mortgage account was up there too.

I hadn't asked them to do it. I didn't have to complete some dreadful online form. It just happened. They thought about what they could do to make my life easier. How great is that? So let me ask you a question. Do *your* customers know that they are your customers? And if they do, do they enjoy that status?

Maybe they just completed a transaction some time ago and, while they might *own* one of your products, don't actually feel a bond with its provider. This is particularly important if you do most of your sales and marketing remotely, through direct marketing or e-commerce, for example. Here are a few things you might do:

- Send them a thank-you letter *every* time they place an order. If logistics prevent you sending it separately, then at the very least you could include it with the order. This is also a good time to make them a further offer, perhaps for a related product, or an extended subscription.

- Ask them for their opinions. In person. Everybody likes this. It makes them feel important and gives them a nice little stroke. You also get invaluable feedback on what you're doing well and what you could be doing better. And please, don't let's kid ourselves that market research surveys do this. They're impersonal, anonymous, and mechanistic.

- Send them a newsletter. But make sure you give them something genuinely valuable. A glossy four-page A4 newsletter is great if it tells them stuff they want to know. Or if it entertains them, makes them laugh, or gives them something to think about.

In practice

- Make your customers feel that you care about them and you have a better chance of keeping them. You don't have to spend a lot of money (though it can help). You do have to think. Hard.

- If you're finding it difficult, the easy answer is to imagine what *you'd* like you to do.

22 DON'T JUST DO SOMETHING, SIT THERE

LET ME ASK you a question. Thinking back over your last full working day, how long did you spend doing just that? Thinking.

a) More than two hours? Oh, come on!

b) Between five minutes and half an hour? More likely.

c) Too busy? You belong to the 99.9 percent club.

The sad fact is that we're all too busy to think. I don't mean that quick daydream about the gorgeous new hunk/hunkette in sales. Or the idle speculation about what you'd do if you won the lottery. No, I mean the creative kind of thinking. Either where you start off from a challenge: "How can I get more business this month?" Or where you just free-associate, wondering about how the world works.

The idea

From a range of conference companies

Think about headlines. Let's take an example. Conference marketing. You may not be involved in this sector but that doesn't matter. Just go with me for a minute or two. Most conference companies (including the ones I write for) tend to use a standard format for their promotions. That extends to the headline.

Suppose you are running a conference on wireless networks. And it's going to be held in 2010. I'm willing to bet my favorite Taylor guitar against your signed Buster Keaton print from *The General* that your headline is . . . wait for it . . .

Wireless Networks 2010

Lest you think I am merely being critical, I should point out that that's what I do for my conference clients. It's in the brief. But what about trying to engage the reader's own imagination? What else could we write? How about . . .

> Give us 24 hours of your time and we'll help your wireless network take wing

> The world's biggest wireless network companies are waiting to meet you

> Golf handicap suffering? Come to Wireless Networks 2010 and improve it
> (Oh, and do a little business too)

And how about your customers? In today's time-deprived universe, many people struggle just to think about what to eat for lunch. Luckily pre-written sandwich menus let them off the hook. But what about business? If all we can manage is to order up "the usual"—another BLT marketing campaign—we are selling ourselves, our business, and our customers short. Which means we need to start thinking again. Wondering. Daydreaming. Letting our synapses flash for a while without expecting "deliverables." So the next time your boss asks you what you're doing. Just tell them. "I'm thinking."

In practice

- Think about a recent piece of copy you wrote. Call the target reader to mind. Now imagine that you *are* that reader.

- Ask yourself, "What would I tell the copywriter about this copy?"; "How does it make me feel?"; and "What does the writer need to tell me to get me to buy?"

ONLINE COPY THAT GROWS YOUR BUSINESS

AH, SPRING. AND a young man's thoughts turn to . . . his garden. Yes, once again I found myself shopping around on the internet for garden stuff. And because it looked like we'd be facing a hosepipe ban that summer, I was after irrigation and water retention solutions. Oops—did I say that? I mean water butts.

I ended up on the Crocus website and, boy, do these guys know how to write well for the web. So well, in fact, that I want to devote this idea to a mini-case study of their copy.

The idea

From Crocus, a gardening website

Crocus have nailed the tone of voice and style that their customers respond to.

Example 1—about plants

> Whatever your garden size or taste, we have put together a style guide to help you to achieve the garden of your dreams, including plants and accessories. Mediterranean, romantic, tropical, child-friendly, scented, take your pick . . .

Lots of "you"s and "your"s there to make the reader feel engaged. And look at those natural, conversational phrases: "Whatever your garden size or taste," "the garden of your dreams," "take your pick."

Example 2—Processing your order

> We know it's an internet tradition but we thought it would be a bit daft to have a shopping trolley in the middle of a gardening site. That's why we've gone for a wheelbarrow. If you see anything you fancy, just click it into the wheelbarrow. That way you don't have to go back and find it when you want to sort out your order.

Again, they let you find out about the buying process at your own pace, rather than trying to hustle you into buying before you feel comfortable. And notice that effortless tone of voice and playful use of gardening metaphors.

Example 3—Keeping shoppers happy

> At crocus.co.uk we guarantee only to send you top notch plants, products, and gifts and will inspect everything carefully before it leaves us to make sure it's in tip top condition. We also do our utmost to package and protect everything so that it doesn't get damaged on its way. However, if you do have a problem, here is what to do:

This copy is from the About Us section of the site. Even though it's addressing a potential negative—a complaint—it manages to sound straightforward and upbeat without being glib.

In practice

- Listen to the people who talk to your customers directly. The good ones, that is. Now write down what they say.

- When you're writing web copy, strive to put as much personality into your copy as possible. Make sure every page sounds like you. Even the privacy policy. *Especially* the privacy policy.

24 (TYPE) SIZE MATTERS

YOU'VE SPENT LONG hours at the pixel face crafting a persuasive narrative about your product. Now you need the message packaged in a form that will interest your customers, making them want to order from you. It's the designer's job to reflect the form and dynamics of the copy in visual terms. And to allow the information to reach the reader's brain with the least obstruction.

How puzzling, then, to observe how many designers apparently strive to achieve the exact opposite. They place as many obstacles in the way of legibility and comprehension as their vanity and advanced technology can devise. (Even more puzzling: designers who do this still get paid.)

The idea

From plenty of companies who should know better

There are many tried and tested methods for a designer to sabotage your efforts to communicate with your reader. Each one of them could ruin your chances of a sale. Here are three:

1. Graphics running behind type, slashing legibility.

2. Low contrast between type color and background, turning reading into a search for a white cat in a snowstorm.

3. Text split illogically over columns or even pages, destroying the rhythm and structure of your copy.

But one of the most common barriers to communication is also one of the most incomprehensible: type set too small to be read with ease. Pretty basic, isn't it? Set your type in a size that can be read comfortably by a normal human being. Yet it's surprising how many designers don't seem to have grasped this most fundamental of principles.

I have even seen the main body copy for a brochure set in a 6-point light sans-serif type—6-point type is for footnotes. Viewed in less than ideal lighting conditions by, say, a 35-year old, it's verging on the invisible.

Take a leisurely look at your fellow humans. Observe how many of them are beyond the first flush of youth and 20–20 vision, and how many of them wear glasses or use contact lenses. A lot of these aging, sentient beings are your customers. They lead busy lives. They have better things to do than wriggling through visual obstacles to reach your sales message.

In practice

- Legibility varies enormously according to font, weight, and line spacing. But as a rule of thumb aim for 9- or 10-point as a minimum size for your main copy.

- Type size does matter. And if the customer can read your message without even being aware of the type size, then it's the right size.

25 | I OBJECT

IF YOU'VE EVER done any face-to-face selling, you'll know something a lot of marketeers and business owners don't. You have to find out not just what will make someone buy from you but what's stopping them from saying "yes."

When you're planning your copy, whether it's a web page, an email, a brochure, or a sales letter, you can't just focus on benefits. [*What? Heresy!—Ed.*] You also have to make a list of all the reasons why your reader might *not* believe you. Might not trust you. Might not buy from you.

Then you have to figure out the answers to all their "Yes, but . . ." questions. Here are three of the most common objections and what to do about them . . .

The idea

From the best direct response ads

Direct response copywriters know something their advertising cousins don't. (Or don't appear to.) You can't make the sale if you've left even a single objection unresolved.

Objection 1—"It's too expensive."

To be honest, price is rarely the real reason why people won't buy from you. It's a smokescreen for deeper-seated objections. Here's what you do. You demonstrate the value of your product to your reader. Show them how much money they'll save, or make, versus the cost. Talk about their purchase as "an investment." That makes it sound more prestigious and introduces the idea of payback.

Objection 2—"I need to talk to someone else."

Here's another classic delaying tactic. So you have to show them what they could lose by hanging back. Time is money, right? And give them testimonials from people just like them—an excellent way to provide that missing conversation and reassurance. Old-school sales guys would imply that, surely, their prospect was the one in charge. "Oh, I didn't realize your wife made all the important decisions."

Objection 3—"I'm not sure I really need this."

If this is what you're hearing, boy, have you got some work to do. It means you haven't sold your product (or service) to your reader. You haven't convinced them that they will be better off with it than without it. Did you cover every single benefit your product offers? Did you explain with facts just how your reader will benefit? Did you tell a story about life with your product that makes it irresistible? No? OK—well, that's your next challenge. You need to take a long hard look at your copy and more importantly at your product. Identify what it does for your reader and this objection will melt away.

In practice

- Itemize every single reason why your reader might not buy from you, however trivial.

- Now answer those nagging doubts systematically and you are closer to your sale.

26 IT CAME FROM OUTER SPACE

Usually, MARKETEERS WHO don't, or won't, overprint envelopes say it's because "Then they'll know it's direct mail." I'm sorry to disappoint these wide-eyed hopefuls, but your reader *already* knows it's direct mail. Unless you're handwriting every envelope and using postage stamps, there are enough clues to give the game away to even the most simple-minded recipient.

Instead, why not try to show them that it's *relevant* direct mail. *interesting* direct mail. Direct mail that could change their lives. You do this with copy. And maybe graphics too. Just as with email subject lines, the outer copy entices you to open it. It arouses your curiosity. It promises some benefit or other.

The idea

From *Radio Times*, a TV and radio listings magazine
The outer envelope for this mailpack covers all the bases. The copy reads, "Your guide to the TV and radio you'll love." There's also a montage of covers. And a flash reading, "Get 12 issues for £1." It's a really powerful come-on to open the envelope. Which is all we need at this stage.

Here's a little example I put together to show you why envelopes are so important.

Suppose you're selling a £130 product by direct mail. You mail 10,000 pieces at a cost per piece of 50 pence. Your total marketing cost is £5,000.

Let's also suppose that you get a 1 percent response rate, i.e., 100 orders. But if we also assume that only 20 percent of people—2,000—actually open your envelope, that's where all 100 orders come from. And your effective response rate is in fact 5 percent. Let's call that your conversion rate.

If it costs you £75 to fulfill each order, your total fulfillment costs are £7,500. So your total costs are £12,500. Your total revenues are £13,000 and your profit is £500.

Now, imagine you find some way of getting 25 percent more people to open your envelope, giving you 2,500 potential buyers. Without increasing your conversion rate, you now have 125 orders.

Your marketing cost is the same: £5,000. Your fulfillment cost has risen to £9,375, making a total of £14,375. Your total revenues are £16,250 and your profit has jumped to £1,875. A 275 percent increase.

And guess how you get more people to open your envelope. That's right! You give them a *reason* to.

In practice

- If you are trying to get renewals for any kind of relationship-based service, use a line of copy that says something like "Important news about your membership."

- Use a photo that dramatizes the fundamental product benefit. If you offer a premium when people become customers or take a free trial, show that with a line promising details of how to get hold of it inside.

HOW WEB 2.0 CHANGES YOUR COPY

WEB 2.0 IS all about user-generated content, social networks, new ways of hooking up with people, and, inevitably, new ways of making money. It also places a premium on truth over hype. Integrity over gloss. Real people over corporate flacks. (Or, to put it another way, the lunatics have taken over the asylum.)

Now this doesn't mean you have to redesign and rewrite your website to emulate the near chaos of many blogs and shared community sites. But maybe you should take a long hard look at your site and ask a few questions.

The idea

From several slick corporate websites

Surf the web for a few minutes and you'll inevitably come across dozens of beautiful yet strangely uncompelling websites. They are too slick, too old-school corporate communications and definitely not Web 2.0 in tone. Here are some questions to run against your own site.

Have we used a slick library image of someone beautiful? (Hint, most people don't relate to these shots because they portray an unrealistic world where every managing director, IT manager, and indeed carpenter is straight out of central casting.)

Have we hidden any trace of humanity? (Hint, without photos of your staff, your principals, or your customers, people are going to start wondering who's really behind your business. Without engaging copy that sounds like a real person wrote it, you're never going to connect with a generation of web users who expect just that.)

Is our copy readable? (Hint, although I did see a pink page with white type and morphing yellow stars on Bebo, most readers are still more comfortable reading dark type on a pale ground. That doesn't move. And is either ranged left or justified. Your designer probably doesn't believe this.)

From now on, every word you write has to be as genuine as the most badly punctuated screed in the blogosphere. As compelling as the item descriptions on eBay. And as involving as the stories posted on social networking sites.

In practice

- Long copy still works for the nano-attention-span crowd, but you've got to work overtime to get them to read it. The easiest way to do it is to use ultra-short paragraphs. And the shortest words you can manage.

- Give your visitors a full and detailed account of the *truth*. In other words, explain exactly why anybody visiting your site should believe a word of what you've said.

THE CASE OF THE MISSING CASE STUDY

I spend a lot of time telling you to focus on benefits in your copywriting. And it's true, benefits make the sale. However, you can bring your benefits to life with a case study. Case studies take time and effort to write. But the impact they make on your website, brochure, or sales pack repays the effort many times over. Why? Because your reader, rightly, perceives the case study as the truth.

Here is where you give them disinterested testimony that your product or service works. Best of all, case studies follow many of the rules of storytelling. You have a protagonist (hero)—your customer. A predicament—the problem or challenge they were facing. A narrative—what you did and why. And a climax—how things turned out.

The idea

From the British Standards Institution (BSI)

A while back I wrote a series of case studies for the BSI that highlighted different areas of their expertise. Each one was targeted at a particular market, and aimed to promote a specific area of expertise. One of the most interesting to write, and I hope to read, was for a Publicly Available Standard (PAS) for vehicle breakdown and recovery.

The client was SURVIVE, a partnership between the motoring industry, motoring services organizations, the Police Service, and Government. Its aim was to improve the safety of breakdown and recovery operators' employees and customers. In partnership with the BSI, it created a rigorous safety standard in six months.

The structure of the case study followed the classic lines described above. I introduced the need for the PAS, then walked the reader through the process, including all the benefits of the standard, and finished by explaining what lay ahead.

When you're writing a case study, here are a few pointers. Try to tell it from your customer's perspective. And use real people, preferably with photos. (Not all clients are happy to give you a mugshot, but always ask.) Include as many *concrete* facts as possible. Explain *specifically* what you did. Use *original* photography wherever possible. Library shots detract from the impression you're trying to create—that this is what happened to a real person or organization.

In practice

- Use quotes from your client. You will need to interview them to get the story and a flavor of their world view. This is an ideal opportunity to introduce a different tone of voice within your still correctly branded case study.

- Ensure that it's clear how the client benefited from your expertise, product, or input. That way you can give your reader a clear idea of how *they* would benefit.

WRITE MORE AND DOUBLE YOUR PROFITS

OUR HOUSE IS stuffed with story books. Some we can read in a few minutes, others take an hour or two. Guess which ones my children prefer? This preference for engagement runs deep in the human psyche. And it may go part of the way to explaining why long copy tends to work better than short copy. In fact, it's been shown that the best copy can double your profits.

Now, many otherwise sane and rational people (you know, marketeers, business owners, people like that) get all huffy when advised that longer copy works better. Yet these are the same sane and rational people who want maximum profits. Hmm.

The idea

From a successful mail order and internet marketing business

Here's another great example of a highly successful business that appears to break the rules about web copywriting. I say "appears" because the "rules" he's breaking aren't rules at all—just myths. I looked at the website of a very successful American marketing consultant and found dozens of long pages including one, picked at random, with 3,072 words of copy.

He's not doing this because he *likes* doing it. He's doing it because it *works*.

Long copy is, in general, more responsive than short copy. This applies to web pages. Sales letters. Emails. Ads. Whatever. Some of the world's most profitable mail-order businesses have tested relentlessly, and ended up with 12-, 24-, or even 32-page sales letters.

For fun? Yeah right! No, for *profit*. "But people don't read that much copy," the cry goes up.

Well, here's the kicker. Maybe they do read it and maybe they don't. Nobody knows. But what we do know is that they *respond*.

Here's my analysis of what's happening. Let's say you have an eight-screen email sales letter. On every screen you include three cross-heads, each one encapsulating, in some way, a benefit. That's 24 benefits-driven headlines. Your reader may well not be reading word for word. But even if they just skim and scan, they are picking up a couple of dozen reasons to buy.

Or you could send them a one-screen email. With three heads. They might not read this one either (a fact often overlooked by the naysayers), preferring to skim and scan. But now they're getting three reasons to buy instead of 24.

That's an 88 percent REDUCTION in selling power.

In practice

- First you have to find out as much as possible about the target reader for the copy. Then you have to dismantle the product until you have a gut understanding not of what it *is*, but of what it *does*.

- Finally you must create a proposition for buying that is so irresistible that once they're hooked, your reader will happily keep reading until you've finished with them.

THERE'S GOLD ON THEM THAR WEBSITES!

ALTHOUGH CORPORATE WEBSITES are fun to design and build—and write copy for—the real work on the web, at least in the commercial arena, gets done on e-commerce sites. Long before the web was invented—or its progenitors conceived—copywriters were staying up late trying to figure out how to part people from their hard-earned in exchange for their or their clients' products.

Now, on Amazon, eBay, and thousands of other e-commerce sites, copywriters are carrying on this proud tradition. Question is, how do you do it? It turns out not to be so very different from the pre-web days, though search engine optimization is an issue (that we'll return to later).

The idea

From an organisation selling collectable gold coins on the internet

My client markets a wide range of collectable coins and gifts—all in precious metals. My brief was to write copy for around 40 e-commerce pages, each one focusing on a particular coin, set or gift.

My job was to give the copy a fresher feel. To make it more web-friendly. And to make it work harder to sell coins. For each of the flagship products, the copy had to follow a new page template developed by the client in collaboration with their web designers.

There are three main sections: an overview, product information, and background and history. To these I added "Thinking of a gift?"—a short paragraph positioning the coin or collectable as a gift and using less technical language.

In the body copy I introduced three key elements for the collector. The theme, "the monarchy." The alloy, "22 carat gold." And the denomination, "five-pound." And technical words to establish rapport with the collector: "conjoint portrait"—meaning two heads. "reverse and obverse"—meaning back and front. I deliberately used the adjective "knowledgeable" to flatter the reader. And also, subtly, to suggest that not buying would be an act of ignorance.

I also used a set of four bullet points, to break up the text and introduce the benefits. Here's one of them:

> Join the ranks of the most serious collectors when you order this rare coin: one of just five bearing a conjoint portrait of the royal couple.

They used verbs, which engages the reader and encourages action. And they stress the exclusivity and rarity of the coin—a big draw for collectors.

In practice

- Whatever you're selling online, write copy that engages the reader's attention instantly. You don't have time to warm them up.

- Use keywords not just because search engine optimization is a good idea, but because reader optimization is an even better one.

31 WHY I HATE TEAMS

Do you remember your fifth birthday? You, know, the one when your parents bought you that really great toy you'd wanted all year. And there was a card with it. Who signed it? Did it say, "Happy Birthday Darling. Lots of Love, The Parenting Team"? Of course it didn't. They put "Lots of love, Mummy and Daddy."

Well, then, what about your first love letter. After a couple of pages of scented pink (or blue) notepaper, crammed with protestations of eternal love, your inamorata signed off with a jaunty, "All my love forever, The Love-You Team." No? You surprise me. NOT!

The idea

From an internet knowledge-sharing network

I joined an internet knowledge-sharing network. It's run by one of the web's gurus of opt-in marketing, yet he makes an elementary mistake in the copy for the welcome email. Here's the opening sentence:

We think we love you!

Wow! How great is that? Really personal and so completely unlike anything you'll get from any other organization. But after a few more paragraphs of similarly inspired copy, here's the last couple of lines:

Enjoy!
Xoxo,
The XYZTeam

Hmm. Something of a pattern emerging here. When we write letters and emails to our friends and family, i.e., the people we have relationships with, we use our name at the end. So why do so many organizations think the way to conclude a "customer service" or "relationship building" email (don't make me laugh) is with some half-hearted "The Watkins Widgets Team"?

Teams are impersonal. Teams can't form meaningful relationships with customers. Teams are anonymous, unaccountable, and just plain wrong. Letters and emails signed by teams say one thing loud and clear: "We don't care about you." Because if they did, they'd have the wit, or the insight, to realize that people like to receive communications from other people. *Individual* people.

If you want to ensure your letter carries the same sort of emotional freight as those birthday cards, love letters, and party emails we all love receiving, go through the text and weed out any references to the reader second-person plural (e.g., some of you), the reader third-person plural (e.g., our customers), or the writer first-person plural (e.g., we).

In practice

- Put the name of the team leader at the foot of the email or letter. Or better still, put the name of someone really important in your company.

- Get them to sign the letter. By that I mean scan in their signature. Do not, ever, use one of those cheapo script typefaces.

"I WANT" DOES GET

READ ANY HALF-decent copywriting book and you'll quickly twig that you're supposed to focus on benefits, not features. What is a benefit? Well, it's anything that makes your reader's life easier or better in some way. Top of my head? Save money. Now, although benefits *will* bring in sales, alone they'll only get you part of the way toward your goal—which should be . . . *maximum* sales.

So what is the missing ingredient? Here's a clue. Why do so many married people get themselves into so much trouble—financial, legal, and emotional—by having affairs? Desire. My dictionary defines desire as an unsatisfied longing or craving. (In its noun form, anyway.) So let's look at what people long for.

The idea

From Carte D'Or, an ice cream brand

If you want to engender desire, you need to make people imagine life with your product. So yes, start by writing down a list of benefits of your product or service. You should definitely include them in your copy. The trick is to couch them in language that reflects your reader's *desires*. Here's some copy from an ice cream ad (accompanied by a full-bleed color photo of the product, which helps):

> The thought of Carte D'Or Chocolate Inspiration ice cream gently melting on top of a steamy chocolate pud is enough to make anyone go gooey in the middle . . . *

* Copy reproduced with kind permission of Unilever.

The words that clinch it for me are "steamy," "pud," "melting," and "gooey": all designed to get the reader's taste buds exploding like fireworks.

When people *want* stuff, crave it, you can bet they'll find a way to get it—even though they patently don't need it. A friend of mine wanted a sports car, even though he could use his wife's car whenever he needed it. Practicality had nothing to do with it. He just wanted it. And take a look at the following list (by no means exhaustive, incidentally) to figure out why.

- Physical pleasure.
- Social acceptance.
- High status.
- Freedom from debt.
- Excitement.
- Risk.
- Physical well-being.
- Respect from others.
- Better family relationships.
- To feel good about yourself.
- Sex (more, better, with different people).

In practice

- A simple technique, well, simple to know about at any rate, is to paint word pictures. They don't have to be long, or flowery, just powerful.

- People often long for stuff they think they aren't allowed to have. So if you restrict supply in some way, you can have them salivating at the prospect of a treat that could be withdrawn. Unless they act *now*.

WHAT DO YOU MEAN "IF"?

33

GET PEOPLE CRAVING or longing for your product (or, to be more precise, feeling that your product can deliver whatever it is they're truly longing for or craving) and you're almost home. But there's still one hurdle you have to leap before you've made the sale. Every sales representative worth their salt knows all about it. Even though it's hard to do. Ready?

You have to ask for the order. So let's talk about the call to action (again). Whatever you're writing, from press releases to Google Adwords, emails to sales letters, you have a commercial goal in mind. That translates into an action your reader must take.

The idea

From a furniture retailer

When you're asking for the order, the trick is getting your reader to take the action using all the word power you can muster. Here's what not to write (from a mail-order furniture retailer) . . .

> If you would like to order . . .

If? IF??? What do you mean "If"?

You've just spent a day, a week, or a month planning, empathizing with your reader, researching your subject, structuring your sales copy, writing the damn stuff, then editing, polishing, and proofreading and you mean to tell me you're allowing them to imagine there's a possibility they won't buy? No. This is no place for the conditional mood. Instead, *command* them to buy. That means using the imperative mood. Like this:

Order today.

Better yet,

Order today and you also receive this package of extra goodies worth £29.99.

Or,

Subscribe now and save 30% off the full rate.

Or,

Register now and bring a colleague along for half-price.

Using the mood of command doesn't mean your reader *will* place that order. But it will push the waverers off the fence, some onto your side. You could go further than the straightforward statement of the product or service being ordered and recap your main benefit and offer. When you're writing your call to action, here's a checklist of language attributes. Your call to action should be:

- Clear.
- Simple.
- Urgent.
- Short.
- Direct.
- Irresistible.

If nobody never asked for nothing, nobody would never buy nothing. [*Er, what?—Ed.*] Oh, all right. In Plain English, if you don't ask, you don't get. Don't be afraid to be specific in asking your reader for what you want. You might be pleasantly surprised.

In practice

- Don't ask for the order, *tell* them to order.

- If you find an errant "If you would like to place an order . . ." at the start of your call to action, delete it and replace with "Order today and you will . . ."

SEND YOUR COPY BY COURIER

No SALESPERSON, ONCE he's discovered a sales secret, will ignore it. He'll take up golf, if that's the game clients like to play. He'll buy them tickets to the opera, even if Speed Metal's more his thing. He'll wear dark suits, if that's what makes the cash register ring.

So what's going on with marketeers? They will cheerfully ignore sales secrets, preferring instead to rely on "intuition," personal taste, or guesswork. The secret I have in mind is, to some eyes, a bit boring. Nerdy even. It has to do with typefaces. One in particular: Courier.

The idea

From Everest, a home improvement company

I receive regular mailings from Everest, inviting me to buy their double glazing. I already have double glazing, so I don't respond. But I notice they always set their letters in Courier. And that means their mailings are hugely more profitable than those of their competitors who use more fashionable typefaces.

Put simply, if you use a serif typeface—like Courier or Times Roman—for body copy, people are five times more likely to understand it thoroughly than if you set it in a sans-serif face like Arial. If you mailshot 10,000 people with a letter set in Arial, it's like throwing 8,000 on the fire yourself. Yet despite the research, this is exactly what happens every day of the week, as well-meaning but dim companies send out mailings in typefaces that they just think look nice.

The best example of this trend is our old friend Courier. Reminiscent of old-school typewritten letters, Courier seems to elicit the most extreme reactions from marketeers. "Ugh!" they say. "I hate it, it looks so old-fashioned." Here's the funny part. Ready?

Letters set in Courier have been shown to be 20 percent more *profitable* than letters set in other, more trendy, typefaces. It's why many of the world's most successful mailings are set in Courier. Some of our clients have tested typefaces and now wouldn't use anything but Courier. Good for them—they're making more money.

Another complaint about Courier is that "it doesn't reflect our brand." So let's take the *New Yorker* magazine. You won't find a single article in Courier within its pages, which groan with advertising for brands such as Mercedes, Lexus, Chanel, and Louis Vuitton. Yet its direct mail letters are set in Courier. Maybe someone at Condé Nast knows something.

In practice

- If you haven't already done so, run a test where you only change the typeface in your mailing letter. Test whatever typeface your designer has chosen against Courier.

- If you're marketing online, ignore all this: there's evidence that sans-serif faces work better on screen.

⬤ TIPS FOR POWERFUL EMAILS

HERE ARE A few of the challenges we face when writing emails. First of all, your recipient can get rid of this intrusion into her working day without lifting a finger. Oh, OK, she does have to lift a finger, but only by four millimeters, before stabbing the mouse button and trashing your promo.

All she needs to do is check out your From field and subject line before deciding that, yep, this is junk mail. (Let's just hope she doesn't consider it the s-word and permanently block emails from you.) If she uses a preview pane, boy have you got a hurdle to jump. As she pages down through her emails, she can see a big chunk of yours without opening it.

The idea

From Which?, a consumer organization

When I registered with Which? Online I received a welcome email, as you do. And although this should be a simple thing to get right, few organizations do. Which? nailed it. The opening's so simple I am always amazed when people forget how to do it:

> Dear Andy
> Thank you for registering with www.which.co.uk.

Then there are a few paras outlining how I log in to the site, what to look out for, how to get in touch if I have a query, and so on. They even tell me to add them to my whitelist so their emails get through. Finally, there's a nice personal sign-off:

Regards
Malcolm Coles
Editor, www.which.co.uk

Yes! Signed by a real person. (See Idea 31 for what *not* to do.)

Here are a few more thoughts on how to write more powerful, engaging emails. Start strong. Give your reader an instant reason to keep reading. What is the huge wow-factor difference your product can make to your reader's life? Give them that. Straight away.

Aim for the most conversational style and tone of voice you can manage without alienating your reader. An email is no place for using "purchase" instead of "buy." And your language needs to be less formal because people are used to the informality of email as a communications medium.

Break up overlong paragraphs. That means virtually all of them. Where do you break them? Wherever it feels OK to do so.

Keep it ultra personal. In direct mail letters, some copywriters feel it's OK to talk about "subscribers," "our customers," or "executives." (They're wrong.) But in an email, which someone might be reading on their BlackBerry or cellphone, you *must* use a personal style to hook them.

In practice

- Remember that email is a personal medium. Strive to replicate the tone and style of the emails your prospects *want* to open. Try using "you" rather than "customers."

- Give your reader lots of chances to order or respond. Not just one at the end.

36 LONG WORDS DON'T ALWAYS MAKE YOU SOUND MORE INTELLIGENT

THERE'S A WIDELY held idea that the more long words you use, and the longer they are, the more intelligent you sound. One of my clients routinely used to talk about supporting people until I pointed out that all they really were doing was helping them. A mild example, but an example all the same.

At its most egregious, this overblown style of writing crushes the life out of its selling message under a sackload of polysyllables. But *sounding* intelligent isn't the same thing as being understood. And in copywriting, if your reader doesn't understand you, they're very unlikely to buy from you.

The idea

From *The Economist*, a business magazine

Trying to come up with a training exercise for a copywriting workshop I was due to run, I flicked idly through a back issue of *The Economist*. Published during the 2008 American presidential race, it had a long article analyzing John McCain and his campaign. I noticed that among the long, sophisticated words and phrases, what we might call high register language, there were an awful lot of very plain, almost slangy words—or low register. Here are the 20 words picked out:

Anathema Bellicosity Blabbing Blokeish Cash Dodgy Embellished Empathetic Fizzy Grumpy Heavies Hindrance Insinuate Misconstruing Nuanced Razzle-dazzle Redoubtable Regurgitating Sizzling Whopping.

I printed them on a worksheet and asked my delegates to split them between those they reckoned came from *The Economist* and those they thought came from *The Sun*, a British tabloid newspaper. It worked beautifully. All the delegates divided the 20 words neatly into two lists of ten. See if you can figure out which way they jumped.

Once I'd had my fun with the "ta daa!" moment, we discussed what *The Economist* was up to, mixing it up like this. (The ability and confidence to use a mixture of registers in the same piece of writing is a characteristic of good literary stylists, according to James Wood, a staff writer at the *New Yorker* and Professor of the Practice of Literary Criticism at Harvard.)

One of the conclusions was that truly intelligent people have no need to show off by using flashy language. Where a longer word is the *only* word that will do, then fine, the writer will use it and use it boldly. But *true* authority, the state of knowing a lot about the subject you're writing about, can just as easily be conveyed through a more muscular, Plain English style.

In practice

- Call a spade a spade, not a cavity construction apparatus.

- If you find you've used a word of three syllables or more, stop for a moment and ask whether there's a one- or two-syllable alternative that means the same.

REASSURING YOUR ONLINE CUSTOMERS

WE KNOW THAT people often abandon an online purchase through fear. It's true. I've done it. Maybe you have, too. And millions of potential online customers continue to do it, every single day.

I don't mean the fear that they haven't understood the point of the animated pile of leaves in a Flash banner ad. Or the terror that comes from trying, unsuccessfully, to read pale gray type on a light blue ground. Or, indeed, the anxiety that arises when they can't find the log-in button.

No, I'm talking about the good old-fashioned fear of making a mistake. They're suffering from what-ifitis.

The idea

From a wide variety of online retailers

Here's a little guide to online buyer psychology. At the point of purchase, many online shoppers are thinking something along the lines of . . .

- What if I click this link and I can't go back?

- What if I give them my credit card details and they pass them on to the Russian mafia?

- What if I don't like what I've bought?

- What if they go out of business tomorrow and I lose everything?

- What if the widow of country X's former energy minister doesn't send me my huge commission after I hand over my bank details? (OK, I made that one up.)

And so on . . .

Your job is simple. Reassure them. Here are a few things you can do. Give them the disinterested testimony of your other (satisfied) customers. Once again, if you don't have any testimonials . . . go out and get some. Give them a little calming pat at every stage of the buying process. Assure them that they can stop or go back at any point.

Have a privacy policy and a prominent link to it on your site. Make your order form/payment pages as clear as you can possibly manage. Then have your Auntie Mary fill them in. If she's worried or confused, go back and take another look. Partner with a reputable payment provider and explain how safe and reliable they are. Offer your customers a money-back guarantee. And sound like you mean it. (Which you do.)

Have a "normal" sounding street address somewhere obvious on your site. It's not that your customers want to come and see you at 123 High Street, Anytown; it's just that they like to feel there's a bricks-and-mortar presence somewhere where they could.

In practice

- Look at every point on your site where you ask your customers to click. Now ask yourself, "Is there an unanswered question here? A what-if?" If there is, then you need some copy to answer that question. Tell them what happens when they click. And tell them what won't happen.

- Have you won any awards for customer service, user-friendliness, or overall reliability? Publish them and get those logos onto your site everywhere where your customers might be doubting your probity.

38 HAVE FUN

MAKING AND SPENDING money is a serious business. How else to account for the numbers of people in prison who took someone else's? Generally speaking, in copywriting circles, humor is treated gingerly. Claude Hopkins, one of the pioneers of advertising copywriting, remarked in his book *Scientific Advertising* that, "People don't buy from clowns."

But does that mean every word we write, every piece of copy we produce, has to be unremittingly serious? I don't think so. You can be playful, witty, provocative even. *If* you know your reader well enough and *if* your style is appropriate to the medium and job that the copy has to do.

The idea

From Malmaison, a hotel chain

A couple of years ago we were staying at the Malmaison hotel in the area of London called Clerkenwell. Home to the famous—and smelly—Smithfield meat market (think large blue plastic barrels with a dozen cows' heads staring sightlessly out at you), it's trendy, a bit bohemian, and stuffed with hip restaurants and bars.

The Malmaison is definitely upmarket but not in a corporate way. We saw no suited execs with wheely suitcases checking their BlackBerrys in the bar. Instead it was full of people who looked as if they worked in fashion, or the arts, media maybe . . . guests at what appeared to be a lesbian wedding . . . and a couple of distinctly rockstar-y types with shades even though the bar was in the basement.

Every single piece of printed material was written in the same consistently offbeat tone of voice. Very personal and quirky enough to reinforce the branding of the hotel itself. Here's the text for the brasserie's comment card (think of the last one you filled in for comparison):

> Thanks for dining in the brasserie today. You were a pleasure. As divine as the onion soup, as cool as the Cloudy Bay. We'd love to hear what you thought of your time at the Mal. Be honest. Feel free to fill in how hot we were for you or any other comments you're bursting to tell us. Thanks for the memories. See you soon.

The tone is distinctive, playful, and engaging. And I think more likely to get the reader to respond than the typical "Your views are important to us" card you see lying aimlessly around in hundreds of hotels and leisure centers. It also flatters the reader, saying, in effect, "We know you're cool and quirky enough to get this; you're not just a run-of-the-mill business traveler."

In practice

- If you're asking for money, I'd stay away from humor and playfulness in favor of a relentless focus on your reader's self-interest.

- But if you have the space and time for a more gentle interaction with your customer, injecting a bit of fun into your copy might just win them over.

39 *THAT* FORMULA

You CAN'T WRITE a book about copywriting without mentioning the most potent formula for writing powerfully persuasive copy: our old friend AIDCA. I discussed it in depth in my last book, *Write to Sell*, but I make no apologies for picking it up again here. You *can* write copy without it, maybe even very good copy. But why go to the trouble?

Even when I don't consciously follow AIDCA, I write copy that turns out to use it as an underlying structure. It's certainly fantastic for planning your copy, allowing you to get all the main elements of your sales pitch down in black and white. You don't have to be a slave to AIDCA, especially not the order, but boy does it help.

The idea

From almost every piece of copy I've ever written (though not all)

AIDCA, as you may well know already, stands for Attention, Interest, Desire, Conviction, Action. As AIDA it's been around pretty much forever, maybe not as an explicitly codified approach to selling, but certainly as a route into a prospect's consciousness, through their objections and toward a sale. When a market trader calls out "Come on girls, lovely fresh pineapples, only a pahnd each!"—he's got all of AIDA right there in that ten-word announcement. And he's been doing that ever since there were markets.

Nowadays, people are more skeptical of sales claims than maybe they were in earlier, less advertising-saturated times. So we add in the C—for conviction. In other words, we aim to convince them that it's safe to act. Or, in other words, that what we are telling them is *true*. Your market trader has it easy. His customer can squeeze, smell, and look at the pineapple to verify that it is indeed lovely and fresh. Copywriters have to work harder in this department. Which is why we rely so much on testimonials, endorsements, statistics, guarantees, and all the rest of the techniques at our disposal.

One thing to say about AIDCA is that you don't have to stick rigidly to it as a *sequence*. With email, for example, it pays to get the call to action in immediately. People may be (only) looking at your copy in the preview pane of their email client. So burying the hyperlink below the fold means you're not giving them any way of responding *at that moment*. Which you should.

In practice

- Gain attention with a headline. Stimulate interest by making your copy relevant to your reader. Engender desire by showing how their life will be improved. Get conviction by proving what you say is true. Secure action by being clear and direct.

- View AIDCA as a checklist rather than a sequence and adapt each message to the circumstances and medium.

IS YOUR COPY FAB?

IT'S TEMPTING WHEN you're selling something to describe it. But this is an elementary mistake made by a lot of would-be copywriters and almost all non-specialists who find themselves facing the task of writing copy about their product. Why is it a mistake? Well, because people aren't really interested in your product. Or you for that matter. Or your company.

What they *are* interested in is themselves. So the way to sell to people is to show them not what your product is, but what it does. And, specifically, what it does for them. This means that instead of describing your product, you have to translate all those features (what it is) into benefits (what it does).

The idea

From MultiTrode, leaders in pump station management technology

Hey, I'm multitasking! As well as writing a book, I'm also writing copy for clients. At the moment, the client I'm working for is MultiTrode. They manufacture clever gizmos that sense and measure water levels and control pumps in all kinds of water tanks. The particular product I'm writing about at the moment is called the Probe. It's packed with features although it's very simple. So I'm using a simple little formula—FAB—to make sure I turn all these facts about the product into benefits for the user—in this case managers of wastewater utilities in Florida.

FAB stands for Features, Advantages, Benefits. Here's an example:

One feature of the Probe is that it has a flexible plastic "squeegee"-type blade attached to the mounting bracket. Another is that it's a smooth cylindrical shape and encased in plastic. As you can imagine (though maybe you'd rather not), wastewater, sewage in other words, isn't just water. There's a lot of other stuff in there too. Let's call it gunk (so we can hold onto our lunch). And this gunk tends to accumulate on any device you suspend in the well into which the wastewater gets pumped.

If you're using alternative sensors, ball floats for example, they get covered with gunk and you have to laboriously scrape or cut it off, using a specially fabricated tool. Yuk. Expensive too, in terms of labor costs.

So, the feature of the Probe is the cleaning blade and smooth outer case. The advantage is that it requires less cleaning altogether and when you do need to clean it, it only takes a couple of minutes. And the benefit is that your workers can spend less time on repetitive and costly maintenance and more time on the things that really matter.

In practice

- Features are what things are. Advantages are how those features make your product better than something else. Benefits are the net result for the customer.

- If you can hear your customer saying, "So what?," you're not talking benefits.

41 SOUTHERN FRIED PLANNING

WHEN I'M PLANNING a new piece of copy, I like to approach reader response from three related directions: what I want them to *know*, what I want them to *feel*, and what I want them to *commit*. Happily, these give me KFC as a little mnemonic. KFC is a tasty little memory-jogger because it drives you to consider your reader as a human being, not just data.

You have to consider what combination of facts and feelings will produce the results you're looking for. And remember that feelings are where all the buying decisions really get made. Sure, your prospects will *tell* you they decided to order because they made a careful evaluation of all the facts; but truthfully? They just felt it was the right thing to do, then went looking for facts to support that feeling.

The idea

From a large food manufacturing company

How many emails do you get in an average work day—20, 50, 100, more? At this manufacturer, their users were sending over 30 million every year. Of those, roughly ten million were cc and not for action. Their employees were also spending around 12,000 hours a week in meetings. That's not particularly exceptional for large companies, but my client wanted to do something about it, so they created a campaign to draw attention to the problem and to modify employee behavior away from sending needless emails and calling unnecessary meetings.

Their HR department hired me to write copy for the campaign. Now, you might think suggesting to busy workers that they spend less time sending or receiving emails or attending meetings would be a no-brainer. After all, everyone's busy so they'd jump at the chance to do less of this stuff. But we needed a strong hook to convince people it was in their interests. After all, it can be a source of pride just how many times your BlackBerry pings in a day (or even in a meeting).

I used KFC to create a framework for the copy. It went something like this:

- I want the reader to Know just how big the problem is and how their own productivity is likely to be affected.

- I want the reader to Feel aggrieved that their time is being wasted and that they have the power to do something about it themselves. And that there's a delicious helping of "me time" being gobbled up by all those meetings and emails.

- I want the reader to Commit to stopping sending unnecessary emails and maybe talking to colleagues instead, and only calling or participating in meetings if there's a clear business reason for doing so.

In practice

- Draw a three-column table labeled K, F, C. Now fill in the columns with the facts, feelings, and actions you want to give, elicit, and get from your reader.

- Beware of false feelings. Feeling that your product is the cheapest on the market isn't a feeling. It's a piece of knowledge.

42 GIVE YOUR READER A KISS

You KNOW THE old management acronym: Keep It Simple, Stupid! Well, apart from calling people stupid (which I don't find very appealing), it's a very useful tool when you're trying to get your message across.

If you have a simple message or a sales pitch for a simple product or service, don't over-complicate it. And if you are selling or promoting a complex proposition, try to simplify it so the reader can figure it out quickly. This isn't dumbing down, just removing all the high walls, barbed wire fences, and flaming hoops a lot of writers erect between their message and their reader.

The idea

From a research consultancy

I did some work for a company that published market reports on different industries and countries around the world. They also had a consulting division, so if you wanted a report on an industry or market they didn't already publish on, they'd put together a custom report just for you. So far, so profitable.

Their main channel to market for the published reports was direct mail. Classic b2b mailings with a sales letter and a brochure. The mailing cost wasn't excessive—around 60p a pop. You'd send out 1,000 and get around 15 orders, which for the time and the conditions wasn't too shabby and paid everybody's mortgage.

Then someone high up had the bright idea that they could generate a whole lot of free leads for the consulting division. The order form on each brochure, hitherto a simple, uncluttered affair "YES! Please send me The Office Furniture Report 2003 @ £595" sprouted an additional, fatal tick box:

☐ Please contact me to discuss a bespoke research project.

What do you think happened to their response rate (that's orders)? If you said, "crashed and burned" you're right. The number of companies ordering the reports fell. (Because they were pondering whether tailored research would be better and deferred the decision to order.) And worse, the expected consultancy leads failed to materialize. Because, I suppose, people who actually wanted tailored research wouldn't read all the way through a mailshot for a published report to get to the order form.

In practice

- In copy terms, be ruthless in reading your copy as if you were the prospect. Ask yourself, "Will they understand me?"

- In commercial terms, don't complicate your order forms. One option of what to buy is best (obviously, this doesn't apply to catalogs). One option for payment is also best (though few do it).

43 SHORT OR TALL?

PRODUCT NAMING ISN'T the only area of marketing where simple word choice can influence sales, but it's a powerful one. A client of mine once showed me an ad for a car whose name, translated into Spanish, was a slang term meaning "wanker."

We all hope to avoid committing that kind of cock-up, but even seemingly OK choices can put people off and depress sales, even when the product itself is fine. In our favorite deli and coffee shop—Bird and Carter—the lattes and cappuccinos come in two sizes: "short" and "tall." Nothing unusual there. To my simple male mind though, it seemed easier to ask for a "large" latte.

The idea

From Bird and Carter, a deli

Co-owner Joff Bird explained to me that his female customers feel happier asking for a "tall" drink rather than a "large" one. Subconsciously, they associate their buying decision with its effects on their figure. So, give your calorie-rich treat a nice, innocuous-sounding name and you sell more. (Except, I suppose, to women over 5′10″.)

It's undeniable that synonyms rarely carry exactly the same shade of meaning. I was coaching some copywriters at a large British charity and the word in question was "expensive." My group were weighing up the alternative, "costly." I pointed out that people are often keen to possess expensive things: houses, cars, clothes, jewellery. Yet offer them something costly and they're likely to balk.

The problem is, I think, that "costly" carries a negative association of "*too* expensive." You can hear someone boasting over dinner that "Yes, it's an expensive suit, but you should feel the quality." Nobody will be crowing that, "I've just bought this really costly suit." In the case of "expensive" versus "costly," you'd do well to choose the latter if, let's say, you were promoting an alternative to "costly" insurance premiums.

Or suppose you were writing copy to sell training courses. You have a basic course and a more advanced course. "Basic" is no good. Your prospect is likely to think, "Well, *I'm* not basic, so I'm not buying." Even though it might be perfect for their skill level. People always want to trade up, *especially* if they're currently at the entry level. So we might retitle our basic course, "Introduction to . . ." or even "Fundamentals of . . ." The product, like our 10oz latte, stays the same, but you give it a name that makes people want it.

In practice

- When you're choosing a product name, ask yourself, "Would I be happy asking for this in public?"

- Try to give your products or services a name that in itself implies the end-benefit, rather than being merely descriptive.

FORGET IMPACT, GO FOR UNDERSTANDING

THERE'S A REAL temptation when designing press ads (or briefing them) to go for high impact designs. Brightly colored headlines, eye-catching illustrations or photography, unusual typefaces or layouts. Yet only one of these will do anything to increase the proportion of people stopping at your ad who can actually understand it. Want to have a guess which one?

If you plumped for the illustrations, well done. Everything else, while full of impact, decreases comprehension of the body copy. Next time you're reading a newspaper or magazine, compare the look of the editorial matter to the advertising. Notice the difference. Unless it's a very trendy new magazine aimed at sk8er boyz and girlz (or something similar), the editorial is mostly set in black type (usually a serif typeface) on a white ground. Not so the ads. Hmmm. I wonder why.

The idea

From Colin Wheildon, the only man ever to have researched and made public the scientific relationship between design and comprehension

That's some build-up, huh? But it happens to be true. Wheildon, a journalist and son of a typesetter, set out to research the effects of different typefaces and layouts on reader comprehension. Wheildon's book is called, in its latest edition, *Type & Layout: Are you Communicating or Just Making Pretty Shapes?*. Buy it. You won't be disappointed. (Your designer might be.)

In it, Wheildon systematically reveals the effects of such art directors' favorite devices as sans-serif body copy, body copy set into unusual shapes, images and captions, ragged versus justified setting, bright color headlines, column width, and so on.

In what is, for me, probably the most telling example, he researched the effects of setting ad headlines in black, versus low and high croma colors (dark blue and bright red for example). Poor comprehension of body copy jumped from 14 percent of research subjects for ads with black headlines to 65 percent for ads with red headlines. Good comprehension dropped from 67 percent to 17 percent when the same color switch was made.

Giving a worked example, he says that if an ad in a national newspaper gains a million readers with a black headline, it will gain 1.6 million readers if you set the headline in bright red. Great, so job done? Er, no. Because, although it has more impact, the red-head ad only delivers 240,000 people who understand it thoroughly, compared to 670,000 for the original. And if they don't read the body copy, they miss the selling message.

In practice

- Color does attract additional readers for your ad, but try using it in non-type elements such as backgrounds or photographs.

- Your designer will probably never have heard of Colin Wheildon and will, in any case, dispute his findings. Run a test.

WHEN YOU DON'T HAVE TIME TO PLAN, PLAN!

My DICTIONARY DEFINES "plan" as a formulated and especially detailed method by which a thing is to be done. When it comes to copywriting, that "thing" could be a letter, email, press release, web page, or any one of the hundreds of media we use to pitch to our prospects. And to me, it seems obvious that you would want to have a detailed method for getting it done.

A commonly held view is that when you are under pressure, the best thing to do when asked to write something is, well, to start writing it. After all, the reasoning goes, the sooner I start, the sooner I'll finish. As we'll see, that statement is holed below the waterline.

The idea

From everything I've ever written

"Early to start means early to finish" is wrong for two reasons. First, if you start like that you won't finish sooner; you'll finish later, because you will need many more rewrites and revisions to get anywhere close to your objective. Second, starting with drafting is not starting at the beginning. It's starting one third of the way in.

The bulk of the work in writing copy is not writing at all. It consists of gaining such a detailed knowledge of your subject that its every aspect is second nature to you. You become so familiar with it that you could sell it face to face to anyone even vaguely interested. That process of research is what leads to those eureka moments when you see exactly why anyone would part with their cash for the product you're selling. The features and how they confer advantages; those advantages and the underlying benefits they deliver.

You also pick up the characteristics of the prospects (your reader, in other words). Their age, sex, attitudes, outlook, hopes, fears, motivations, spending power, way of talking, favorite reading material . . . whatever it is that defines them.

Having got to grips with whatever it is I'm selling, I need a route map for the document I'm writing. This is where I divide up the writing between the various points I want to make, the sections I'm going to need, my opening, call to action, PS, and response device. Only when all this is in place do I feel confident enough to begin the task of choosing words and arranging them on the screen.

In practice

- Don't kid yourself that you can write without a plan. You *will* need to spend time thinking before you start writing. That's planning.

- Create a written plan for each document you write. Bullet points, Post-Its, spider charts, it doesn't matter. Find what works for you.

"I JUST NEED TO MAKE ONE MORE CHANGE"

THE DESIRE TO write the perfect sentence was so strong that Marcel Proust used, reputedly, to take a year to write one. (OK, I made that up. It may have been more like an hour.) For many novelists that's a luxury they don't feel they can afford or need. For copywriters, too, it's a source of conflict.

On the one hand you want to turn in a flawless piece of copy (we'll assume for a moment such a thing exists); on the other, you have a commercial imperative to get the thing out there into the marketplace and see if it works.

The idea

From a corporate brochure I wrote for a large international company

It was 11.30 a.m. in London, 6.30 a.m. in New York and 8.30 p.m. in Tokyo. In each of those three cities sat a participant on a conference call to discuss the corporate brochure I was writing. I drew the long straw; I was in London sipping a mid-morning coffee. The draft in front of us was number 11. I'd like to think that this was not because of any fault in the writing (well, I would say that, wouldn't I?), and more to do with the conflicting desires of the two regional barons on the call with me.

My role in the call was ostensibly to take notes; it was rather more about conflict resolution. Long stretches passed where I listened as Tom and Nick (not their real names) tore into each other's concept of what the brochure was for and what it should sound like. Down the line from a Tokyo hotel room came crackling instructions from baron number two on the sort of organizational chart that would best represent the business. These would be batted back from downtown Manhattan as baron number one asserted his alternative concept.

My chance came as the combatants drew breath. "Wouldn't it be better," I asked, "to just print a couple of thousand and just get it out there? This thing will never please both of you and meanwhile your competitors have the field to themselves." In the end we did get sign-off and we did print it. In a version neither man was happy with but which both felt represented a partial victory over the other.

In practice

- Understand that copy is a tool not an art form. Its job is to sell stuff. Perfect copy doesn't exist, any more than do perfect employees.

- Keep to a minimum the number of people with final approval, preferably to one. Get them to sign off the brief, so the copy, when it comes, meets their stated expectations.

ANOTHER HEADLINE IDEA: TRUE OR FALSE

HEADLINES ARE PRETTY near the top of every copywriter's "most difficult to write" list. Along with openings for sales letters and believable customer stories. Everyone knows that the best kind of headline is the one that appeals directly to the reader's self-interest— promises a benefit, in other words. OK, not everyone, but everyone who's ever read a book about copywriting.

But that formula only takes you so far. "Yes, but what can I actually *write*?" is the plaintive cry. Here's a little trick you can try next time. Especially if you have a proposition that is unexpected, unknown, or new.

The idea

From the London Stock Exchange

The proliferation of rules, regulations, and financial opportunities for listings on global stock exchanges means even seasoned finance directors and CEOs need a bit of help identifying the right thing to do. My client at the time, the London Stock Exchange, had a flyer in mind that would at once educate its clients about a new opportunity and persuade them to list their American depositary receipts (ADRs).

The approach we took was to pose a question that addresses potential ignorance head-on, without making the reader feel stupid. It read:

True or false: you can list ADRs in London?

It worked on a number of levels. People like solving this type of puzzle. For finance directors looking for an exchange on which to list their ADRs, it promises a benefit—that they could do it in London, a major world financial center but not an American one. And the statement after the colon is presented in positive language—you can list ADRs in London—so if the headline is all you read the lingering memory is of the right answer: yes you can.

Because the piece was presenting a new concept, we opted for a very straightforward, non-ritzy selling approach. I included six reasons to take the desired action—the benefits. Then a box containing four key facts about listing ADRs. Then a testimonial. Then a Q&A section presenting, apparently dispassionately, further reasons to do it and resolving any objections in the reader's mind.

In practice

- You can flip the copy around, starting with the concept you're presenting and ending with . . . true or false? For example, "You can lose weight without giving up cream cakes, true or false?"

- Start your body copy with a two-word sentence: "It's true." Then go on to explain why.

BE DIFFERENT

PICK ANY CATEGORY of copywriting—promotional emails, flyers, mailshots, e-zines—and it's a fair bet that the last 50 examples you've seen (let's not say written) are, effectively, the same. Same format, same structure, same style, even the same benefits. Which is a bad thing. Why?

Because our readers, poor suffering souls, get hit with this stuff day in, day out. And it's boring. Somebody once asked me in a copywriting workshop why it was a bad idea to start a letter to customers, "As a valued customer." "I got one this morning that started like that," she said, "from an online chocolate retailer. And one yesterday." My point exactly.

The idea

From a government department

BLU (sadly no longer around) was a business unit with the Small Business Service of the Department of Trade and Industry. Got that? It provided publications, events, knowledge management, and networking to the myriad organizations in Britain that themselves support enterprise, from chambers of commerce to local outfits called Business Links. Our job as their marketing agency was to write, edit, design, and print . . . everything. Flyers, emails, ads, white papers, reports, mailshots, posters, certificates, you name it.

Trouble is, there was an awful lot of printed material flying around "the network" at the time and information overload was an ever-present danger. When one particular working party finished its research program, we decided on a different approach. Rather than produce yet another traditional-looking report, we hit on the idea of creating a magazine. A one-off publication that borrowed all the techniques magazine publishers employ to fight for attention on the news-stand and in the reader's home.

The cover featured a series of cover lines including "47 Ideas to Increase the Value of Learning Groups." Instead of having sections, we wrote and laid out the conclusions as discrete articles with titles including "What have Alcoholics Anonymous and Weight Watchers got to do with business support?," "Beyond the cheesy pineapple," and "Action learning for CEOs." Then there were pull quotes, where we picked a good quote from the body of an article and blew it up as a panel; bylines, i.e., each author's name by their article; standfirsts—the bit of copy between the headline and the start of the body copy; and lots of full color illustrations and photos.

It got rave reviews, requests for multiple copies, and, most important of all, read.

In practice

- When you're writing or designing a marketing piece, don't just do what you did last time, or, worse, what your competitors are doing. Look further afield: at other markets, other industries, other media altogether.

- Do remember why you are writing, though: "creativity" just becomes hot air when it floats free of its commercial moorings.

UTILIZE LEXICAL ECONOMY, ER, I MEAN USE SHORT WORDS

I'VE JUST READ an article about inaugural speeches given by American presidents. The comment that leaped out at me was that Abraham Lincoln, the best writer and deliverer of such speeches, would never use a three-syllable or even a two-syllable word where a one-syllable word would do.

Some years later, in 1946, George Orwell wrote, in his essay "Politics and the English Language," that scribes should not use a long word where a short word will do. It's instructive to compare the sentiments of these two giants of the English language to those espoused by the pygmies inhabiting many so-called communications departments. Here we find a rule that Orwell might have described as, "Four beats good, Two beats bad."

The idea

From a couple of corporate websites

I came across a great example of corporate speak recently on the website of a large consulting firm. They advertise proudly that, "Our specialization is the provision of business solutions." Whatever that means. Another's home page was so dense that it achieved a Flesch Reading Ease score of zero. To put that into perspective, the American Internal Revenue Code is easier to understand.

It's fairly easy to imagine the process in the writer's mind that leads to this sort of sludge. "We're an important firm with lots of extremely clever people working for us. And our clients, equally, are very senior people. To demonstrate our cleverness we will use the longest words we can find, even when describing the simplest of concepts." That may be according them more respect than is their due. The reality, I suspect, is more likely to be that the writer simply likes the *sound* of all those long words floating around on their screen.

This, I'm afraid, simply will not do. We are not children, to be comforted or amused by pleasing sounds, any more than by flashing lights or bright colors (see under Flash animation). There is a job to be done here, an important job. It's called communicating. And the best way to communicate an idea accurately from one brain to another is to use the shortest words you can. So, our hapless consultants might have said, "With what we've learned about all businesses, we can solve the problems in yours." Not all one-beat words, but more than enough to beef it up and convince the reader it's worth reading on.

In practice

- Wherever you've written a word with more than four syllables, strive to replace it with a punchier, shorter alternative.

- Don't follow the rule slavishly. The ultimate guide is to choose the best word for the job.

50 ALMOST UNIQUE

"Unique" is one of a small but powerful group of words characterized by their magnetic appeal to a certain type of copywriter. Other members of this lexical junta include "fantastic," "exciting," "amazing," and "delighted." As in, "I am delighted to inform you of an exciting new development at XYZ company." Like we care.

Paradoxically, the products I've seen that could truly claim to be unique rarely do so. Perhaps the copywriter didn't notice. Or was unequipped with enough research to discover it. Then there are all those wonderful moments where we find humdrum products described, variously, as "quite," "almost," and "one of the most" unique.

The idea

From a legal publishing firm

A client of mine publishes legal textbooks. The one I have in mind covers the reinsurance market. Reinsurance is that "belt and braces" business where insurance companies take out insurance policies on the risks they're insuring. I'm not sure who insures the reinsurers. Anyway, back to the point. The two major world centers for reinsurance are London and Bermuda.

My client's book is the only one to cover the reinsurance market in depth in both jurisdictions. And as we know, when the word "only" appears, the word "unique" can't be far behind. That single feature provided the platform for the whole brochure, from strapline to headline, body copy to call to action. It worked because it was a) true and b) a compelling benefit to the customer, who would only need to buy one book (they're not cheap).

When you start a new assignment or project your first job is to interrogate the product. In other words, to find out as much about it as there is to find out. Sometimes that's easy. There are spec sheets, press releases, or previous ad campaigns to review. Then there are the limitless possibilities of the web, from Wikipedia to newsgroups, blogs to Google. Ah, dear Google, what did we do before there was you?

From your research you may well find out one unique thing about your product. It's worth talking about, especially if you can find a way to make it sound like a benefit to the buyer. In any case, laying out *why* it's unique is a whole lot more interesting than just slapping the old "unique" sticker on it and hoping some mug will go "Ooh! Look—unique."

In practice

- Do your research. Read anything and everything you can discover that relates to your product. Recently, I found myself on the American Environmental Protection Agency website, downloading PDFs that were exactly what I needed.

- Remember that your reader has seen everything described as "unique" and therefore believes nothing is. Prove it's true.

51 FIND YOUR CUSTOMER'S PAIN POINT

LOTS OF PRODUCTS and services are there to make people's lives easier in some way. Not more pleasurable, necessarily, just less unpleasant. Life insurance being an obvious example. Loft insulation another. As copywriters selling this type of product, we need to be looking for our customer's pain point—not to inflict it, but to remove it.

Business-to-business markets in particular are stuffed with this type of thing, a reflection I suppose of the extraordinary pressures modern business imposes on its participants. Losing money, employing crooks (by accident, not on purpose), breaking rules, being fined, getting sued, having secrets stolen, losing pitches, being rejected: they're all points of pain. And that makes them excellent motivators.

The idea

From the World Advertising Research Center, a marketing data company

WARC used to publish a series of brilliant little data books on all kinds of markets and industries. They're pocket sized but stuffed with as much data as books ten times their size. This benefit is summed up in the strapline "Heavyweight data in the palm of your hand." Nice, huh? For a mini catalog, promoting the whole range, we came up with the line "Plan, pitch, presentation? Here's your supporting data."

The point of pain being the fear that naturally accompanies anyone who has to prepare a plan, make a pitch, or give a presentation. What if I've missed something? What if the opposition have better data in their pitch? What if I stand up to speak and the audience knows more than I do? If you've ever had to write a business plan, take part in a competitive pitch, or give a speech or presentation, you'll recognize those ghastly 3:00 a.m. questions.

WARC's pocket books promised (truthfully) to give the customer the data they needed to make those questions go away. Or at least recede to the point that they could get a decent night's sleep.

You need to handle this approach with a light touch of course. Spend too much time harping on about all that pain and your prospect identifies with the problem not the solution. Plus the mere act of reading your copy is now making them feel that pain all over again. The easy way out for them is not to order but to stop reading.

In practice

- You can start an email or letter, "Have you ever wished that . . ." or "If you've ever wished that . . ." followed by the point of pain evaporating.

- The next para starts, "Well, now you can. Thanks to a new scientific discovery, piles are a thing of the past."

ANOTHER HEADLINE IDEA: USE "HOW . . ."

JUST BEFORE REOPENING this document I took a phone call from a freelance writer who specializes in business and technology journalism. She was talking about how she looks for headline ideas. "I often look at song titles," she said. You know the sort of thing. "Stairway to Devon" for a travel magazine. "Smells Like Green Spirit"* for an article on a new apple-flavored liqueur. "You've got the red-nose pain, dear" for a piece on sinusitis.

In editorial writing, headlines share part of the job they do in sales writing: enticing the reader to read on. But there's rarely a need to sell, so the emphasis is on the article's content, not on any benefit of reading. There is a common approach that works. It's to use "How . . ."

The idea

From Dale Carnegie, Stanley Kubrick, and others

One of the, if not *the*, best-known self-help books ever published, and certainly one of the first, was Dale Carnegie's *How to Win Friends and Influence People*. It's such a great title, quite honestly, they might as well have just printed the title, the price, and a toll-free number and started reeling 'em in. Then, there's Stanley Kubrick's cold war masterpiece, *Dr Strangelove or: How I Learned to Stop Worrying and Love the Bomb*. What is the enduring power of How? It has to do with what comes next.

* In a weird moment of synchronicity, as I write this idea on a train, the lady opposite me is reading *Soldier: the Magazine of the British Army*, and one of the cover lines reads TEEN SPIRIT.

You either give an explanation:

How to make more money in a month than most people make in a year

Or a story:

How I discovered the secret of looking younger for longer

Or a promise:

How you can retire at 40

At any rate, it occupies the gold-laden subsoil called Practical Advice. Dig down a few feet and your spade clangs on a cabbage-sized nugget that will make you or your client rich.

People are intrigued by "How" headlines. They want to know what comes next. If you've chosen the right problem, or the right dream for your prospect, "How" allows you, almost forces you, to engage them with your body copy. Practical advice is a useful thing. Models want advice on staying thin. Anglers want advice on catching monster carp. Athletes want advice on the best training regimes.

In practice

- When writing a "How" headline, remember to link the advice to a problem relevant to your reader. Offering to tell monks how to make a million probably won't entice them to read on.

- Make it personal by using a "How you could . . ." opening.

WE'RE NOT SELLING TO *YOU*

I WAS IN a meeting with a client last week and the conversation turned to their in-house copywriters. "The trouble our junior marketing executives have," said the marketing manager, "is that they find it hard to understand what it's like being one of our customers." And that nails one of the top challenges we all face: getting inside our prospect's or reader's or customer's head. Feeling life the way they feel it. Sharing their problems.

But that's what we get paid for: our ability to empathize with our reader—then sell to them. So how frustrating to come up against a manager (or, occasionally, a client) who tells us to change the copy because, "I wouldn't respond to that."

The idea

From BBC Magazines

When we won a pitch to create a raft of marketing communications for this well-known magazine publisher, there was much fist-pumping and high-fiving at Sunfish Towers. (Oh, all right, we said, "Well done, Sir," and "Yes, I thought that went rather well.") Imagine it: a stable of titles, some of which I was already subscribing to, covering subjects I love including cars, gardening, and cooking.

Now, for the car title, empathizing with the target subscriber was easy. It was me. A 40-something bloke of reasonable means who spends a good part of the time (when not scribbling away) filling his dream garage with exactly the right selection of four-wheeled exotica. But what about the cooking title? In a stroke of briefing genius, the editor called her readers, non-disparagingly, "suburban." With just that word she unlocked the puzzle for me. Suburban women who see cooking as a chore for most of the time and an anxiety inducing headache when dinner parties loom.

The publishers, editors, and marketing managers at the client never say, "Well, I wouldn't respond to that" because they know the big secret. "We're not selling to you." They might say, "I don't think our readers would use a word like that." Which is fine. More than fine, in fact, as it gives me a steer in the right direction to hit the appropriate tone of voice that will make a connection with the prospect.

In practice

- If you're writing copy, be ready to justify why you chose a particular word or phrase in terms of its impact or relevance to the reader.

- If you're approving copy, *judge it as if you were the prospect*, not the boss. It might offend your sense of taste, or aesthetics, but you're not the one being sold to.

GIVE YOUR READER SPACE TO THINK

THERE'S A TEMPTATION, when writing for print communications, to want to cram as much in as possible. After all, the reasoning goes, we've paid to get this mailshot/brochure/white paper printed and mailed, we're damn well going to fill up every square inch. The picture online is more confused, but you still see plenty of emails, banners, and landing pages that scream for the reader's attention.

But does this approach work? Long copy does sell, we know that. So should we stuff the page with words like a Périgord goose being force-fed corn to turn its liver into foie gras? Well, no. Your reader needs a little breathing space. Somewhere calm to consider your argument.

The idea

From Waitrose, a supermarket

Actually, describing Waitrose as merely "a supermarket" is a bit like describing a Bentley as "a car." It's a lovely supermarket. A super(up)market if you will. (I'm a fan as you can probably tell.) In our neck of the woods we're fortunate enough to have their flagship store. Wander around and the feature of the store that strikes you is the aisles. Wide? Yes, I suppose that covers it. In fact they're wide enough to drive the aforementioned Bentley down them without knocking over the merchandise.

You feel calm. You feel happy. You feel like browsing along the shelves and picking up that actually quite reasonably priced jar of feta-stuffed peppers. You go in looking for a loaf of bread and a couple of apples. You come out £150 lighter in the back pocket having also picked up a dozen luxuries, a DVD player, and some artisan-produced, sustainably sourced clothes pegs. But you don't mind. They made it feel like pleasure.

The wide aisles in Waitrose are the retail equivalent of white space. What's white space? It's the places on your promo without words. Or graphics. Or anything at all. Its job is to give your words space to work their magic. The reader doesn't feel hemmed in or crushed under looming towers of tightly packed sentences. No. It's altogether a more relaxing experience. And because you linger, you spend more.

In practice

- For anything even vaguely upmarket, plan on allowing the designer at least 25 percent of the available real estate to play with—50 percent would be better.

- If you find you've written so much copy it fills the page, persuade whoever's paying to pay for more paper. Or go onto a new screen. Or edit it down.

55 LET'S PLAY 20 QUESTIONS

I WAS IN a meeting with a potential client once, discussing a new piece of marketing literature. The aim was to produce a sales tool for their distributors' telemarketing staff. We started discussing possible content and the potential client said, "We want to include a section on handling objections." I asked them what the typical objections to buying their service were. There was a silence.

It transpired that they had no idea why people might not want to buy their product. In fact, they weren't altogether sure why people *did* buy their products. Back to the drawing board. And that set me thinking about my own career in marketing, including six years directing a marketing department.

The idea

From my own career in sales and marketing

It wasn't until I started meeting and speaking to customers that I truly began to understand what motivated them. I used to write copy back then, too. And believe me, it became a lot easier once I could hear those voices telling me not just why they did buy, but why they might not. So here are some questions you might want to ask *your* customers, before you start that next piece of copy.

1. What does your job entail?
2. How is your performance measured?
3. What kinds of decisions do you have to make and how often?
4. When you make those decisions, what sort of information do you need first?

5. What do you do with that information?
6. Is there one thing that would make your life easier right now?
7. What is it?
8. Would you consider buying that thing from us?
9. If not, why not?
10. When you are considering buying a product like ours, what are you looking for?
11. And what are you not looking for?
12. Is price important?*
13. When you're using one of our products, what do you get out of it?
14. Is there anything you'd change about it?
15. What's the most important thing you need to know before deciding to buy?
16. What else do you want to know about our product?
17. When considering buying one of these products, whose opinion would make you feel more secure in your decision?
18. Do you buy things from other suppliers that you'd consider buying from us?
19. Have you ever nearly bought one of our products and then changed your mind?
20. If so, what was the reason?

In practice

- Don't assume you know why people buy your products. Find out. In person.

- Hanging out at user groups online is an excellent way to get unvarnished opinions. Take your thick skin with you, though.

* You'd be surprised how often the answer is "no."

56 OPTIMIZE FOR YOUR CUSTOMER FIRST

IF YOU WRITE for the web you'll be very familiar with the abbreviation SEO. Search engine optimization is an obsession for some companies, rightly so, since without those all-important top spots on Google (and the others) they're losing business. You can read books about SEO copywriting, subscribe to SEO copywriting e-zines, read blogs focused on SEO copywriting, and, generally, gorge yourself on advice about how to get SEO copywriting right.

But you need to be subtle about it at the same time. If you spam the search engines two things happen. One, they're likely to down-rate your site or blacklist it altogether and two, your visitors, assuming you still have any, will turn away in disgust.

The idea

From Nick Carpenter, boss of Oxford New Media, a digital marketing agency

Nick is my go-to guy for all matters web-related. He designed and handles distribution of my e-zine and advises me on digital marketing. Incidentally, Nick once told me my website does all the wrong things in terms of SEO . . . but it still gets the top spot for the keywords that I care about. Testament to my copywriting skills rather than my facility for website design, I guess.

We were discussing SEO copywriting one day and he gave me this simple little mantra that I repeat under my breath when writing web copy: optimize for the customer first and search engines second. Otherwise you get stuff like this:

If you need widgets, you need to get your widgets from Watkins Widgets of Wolverhampton. Red widgets, blue widgets, plastic widgets, steel widgets, whatever the widget, we have the right widget for all your widget needs.

Sky-high keyword density, subterranean reader engagement.

As they say, you can lead a horse to water, but you can't make it drink. In this case, your search engine ranking leads the horse, but it's the copy that makes the equine imbibe. Another reason to optimize for your customer is that they won't simply check out the top spotted site, they'll visit a handful, maybe dozens if the buying decision warrants it. So focusing only on SEO means you come across badly when they start reading your copy on the page.

In practice

- Yes, you need to weave your keywords into your copy—in page titles and tags as well as the body copy itself—but make sure that the finished page engages the reader once they arrive.

- Try reading your copy aloud. Moronic repetition of keywords will show up in an instant.

57 USE STORYTELLING TECHNIQUES

I'M THINKING OF a time before BlackBerrys, before email, before PowerPoint. Before PCs, pencils, movable type, quill pens, or even woodcuts. Yes, the Bronze Age. What do you mean, you didn't guess? We were still great communicators then. Fantastic communicators, some of us. Know which ones? The storytellers.

It's part of what makes us human. The love of stories is transmitted if not genetically then as near as you can get. And storytelling is a great tool for copywriters. I wrote in my first book, *Write to Sell*, about a proposal I helped write using story techniques. It had a great title too: "The day I nearly died: a true story."

The idea

From Hamleys, a toy shop

Hamleys commissioned me to write a microsite a couple of Christmases ago. The main page was a history of Hamleys from its opening in 1760 to the present day. Here's the opening line of the copy:

Once upon a time a boy dreamed of owning a toy shop.

Now Hamleys could have gone down the boring corporate route with a line reading "Hamleys has been the world's favorite toy shop for over 240 years." But that would have been a boast, not a story and Hamleys is all about the greatest story of them all: the story of dreams, and of childhood.

The copy draws heavily on fiction techniques, such as engaging more than one sense. We all liked the line: "Over the street-sellers' calls and horses' hooves ringing on the cobbles, you could just make out the delighted cries of children as they approached the window." Maybe a tad schmaltzy but it fits the brand and the context perfectly.

In classic storytelling structure, the copy takes the reader on a journey alongside the protagonist: Hamleys. There are challenges: the Depression in 1931 and the Blitz. And a resolution to these, as the store was rescued by a white knight in the shape of Walter Lines, the chairman of the Tri-Ang company. And, because it *is* a toy shop (and my client), a happy ending:

> The toys may have changed, but if he were here today, we're sure William Hamley would recognize the same delighted faces as he guided you round the shop he dreamed of as a boy.

In practice

- To tell a compelling story you need four things: a hero, a problem, a narrative (what happened), and a resolution (the ending).

- Try it with the About Us page on your website: so much more interesting to write—and read—than the "We are the leading blah blah blah."

58 LOOK AT ME! I'M SMILING AND POINTING AT A LAPTOP

I HAVE FIVE box files in a cupboard next to my desk. They're filled with mailings and brochures I've collected over the years. Some because they're interesting, amusing, well written or designed, novel, or just plain odd. And then there's the Black Museum. In the Black Museum is a collection of marketing materials that we call, technically, *crapismus maximus*.

They gain entry into the hall of shame for all sorts of reasons but one of the most common is the use of trite imagery. I have written on this subject before, and will again, but it's those smiley businesspeople. Just one question for those who commission, approve, and print/upload them. Why?

The idea

From a firm of printers who mailed me a lovely example for the Black Museum

Ah yes. Here we are again. It's the marketing manager of XYZ Printing Company Ltd in conversation with his designer.

> "I want to show how our company is professional. You know, not just a bunch of hairy-arsed printers in a factory in East London."

> "OK," says the designer. "How about we source some images of business types in a meeting. They'll make you look really smart because people will associate them with you."

Be honest. How many times have you . . .

a) Sat with a couple of colleagues, smiling at a computer monitor, while one of you actually touches a pie chart on screen?

b) Stared into the middle distance, sucking pensively on one end of your designer glasses frame, while standing by a venetian micro-blind taking in the view over that beguiling mistress we call The City?

c) Taken part in a meeting with a group of five impossibly good-looking people where you all laughed and showed off your very white teeth.

None? I'm not particularly surprised. Want to know why? Because . . .

a) Nobody ever does that. It's a stupid thing to do.

b) You're too busy. (And your office looks out onto a main road. Or a ventilation duct.)

c) People who are that attractive work as models.

And, in fact, that's my point. Those stock library shots are always posed by models. Of course they are: that's their job. But they don't look anything like real purchasing managers. Or lawyers. Or marketing executives. So why do so many companies produce websites/brochures/ads populated with these twinkly eyed, buff-bodied "businesspeople"? I suspect they harbor a subconscious desire to appropriate just a little of that glamor for what they perceive to be their own rather humdrum products.

In practice

- Why not take photographs of *your* customers. Or *your* staff. Doing what real customers and real staff do.

- Caption them in a way that reinforces your positioning and copy points.

THE RIGHT WAY TO USE NUMBERS

FOR SOME PEOPLE, the mere sight of a headline is enough to set off their bulls**t detector. "I can spot marketing speak a mile off," they confidently assert. These are the people who assume that all advertising is lies and that people like me are somewhere below pond life in the intellectual food chain. But . . .

Show them the same sales pitch converted into numbers and a fair few of them will, magically, be transformed into believers. "Did you know," they now equally confidently assert, "more than three-quarters of golfers who switched to the Heavy Helga driver now hit the ball 87 percent further?" Nice.

The idea

From *the Times Higher Education*, a newspaper

Media kits are almost the perfect vehicle for numbers-based copywriting. Advertisers, and their agencies, need to know, in detail, how many people read or otherwise consume the media outlet being promoted. They want demographics, shopping habits, income, preferred reading . . . you name it, the media kit has to provide it. (Although I did see one that, in essence, said, "You can reach posh people when you advertise in [title]." Judging by the ads they carry, it works.)

For the *Times Higher Education* (*THE*), we wrote and designed a media kit that drew on an extensive reader survey. Our job was to convey the attractiveness of the proposition—advertising in the *Times Higher*, as it's known—without drowning in statistics.

So, we gave percentages, "93 percent of Higher Education and university staff read *THE* because it's easy to read." "*THE* readers authorize the purchase of 87 percent of all student books." "80 percent prefer *THE* for job information."*

We also expressed the numbers graphically, because for a lot of people, pictures are easier to assimilate than percentages. If you say 25 percent, it takes longer for your reader to process than if you show them a cake with a quarter cut out. In fact, this is a good point to remember: wherever you can, unless you're writing a technical document or for statisticians or economists, express percentages as fractions. Prefer two-thirds to 66 percent; three-quarters to 75 percent, and nine in ten to 90 percent.

Numbers have a precision about them that words alone can often lack. This precision, for most people, lowers their resistance to taking in the rest of your message. It's far more effective to talk about "savings of £32.74" for example, than "great savings."

In practice

- Whatever you're writing about, try to discover at least a couple of facts that can be expressed numerically.

- When talking about money, cash values resonate more than percentage savings. (You can hedge your bets by quoting both. I do.)

*Figures reproduced with kind permission of the *Times Higher Education*.

ASK YOUR READER A QUESTION

WHAT DID YOU have for lunch yesterday? You just stopped reading and thought, didn't you? Questions do this. It's what they're for. In conversation, they're how we elicit information from the person we're talking to. In the simulated conversations we create in our copy, they're a means of engaging a reader who, initially, may be indifferent, bored, or downright hostile.

As we can't hear their answer, it's pretty one-sided, but it does stop them, momentarily, from deleting or binning our copy. And in that instant, we have the chance to capture their attention. For that reason, I use them a lot. In everything from press releases to sales letters. Especially in sales letters.

The idea

From the Landscape Design Trust, a charity concerned with public space

To promote their magazine, *Green Places*, the Landscape Design Trust wanted to revamp their existing leaflet and asked me to inject a more engaging tone of voice. The first thing I did was to turn the opening around from one that lectured the reader to one that asked them to engage with it and, by extension, its subject matter. Here are the opening three paragraphs . . .

> Are you engaged in public space? Do you want to keep abreast of new developments in the this fast-changing sector? Are you interested in what your colleagues in other disciplines— from landscape architects to green space managers—are thinking, and doing?

Ten times a year, *Green Places* helps you explore new ideas and best practices in public space. It is a news briefing, a reference source, a forum for debate, and something more . . .

. . . your connection to the people, the ideas and the activities shaping—and reshaping—our public spaces.

Because we already knew, from the list selection, that everyone reading was engaged in public space, the answer had to be yes, a nod, in other words. And who could answer no to the second question? Another nod. The same held true for the third question. Get your prospect to nod three times and they are more likely to agree with you when you ask for the order.

You see headlines using questions all over the place. A favorite of mine—and a long-running one, which always tells us a lot—reads, "Would you like to be a writer?" For those who do, it's a winner. The promise is dangled right in front of their nose and they aren't nodding, they're shaking their head so vigorously it's in danger of coming loose.

In practice

- Try starting your next piece of copy, an Adword, a report, a letter, with a question. In fact, try opening with three.

- Pick your questions carefully. The answer must be yes.

61 ⬤! YOU FLATTER ME!

Benjamin Disraeli, nineteenth-century British novelist and Prime Minister, once observed that, "Everyone likes flattery; and when you come to Royalty you should lay it on with a trowel." He might have made a good copywriter. Although we profess to despise flattery, and the flatterer (in *Timon of Athens*, Shakespeare has Apemantus rebuke a fawning poet with the lines, "He that loves flattery is worthy o' th' flatterer"), we are nonetheless pleased whenever we receive any.

This technique is useful for lowering your prospect's resistance to your message. Suggesting that they must be unusually perspicacious, handsome, wealthy, or otherwise endowed is unlikely to meet with disagreement. In that moment, you have the chance to press on.

The idea

From *The Field*, a country sports magazine

What fun, writing a mailshot to sell subscriptions to *The Field*. Guns, dogs, horses, countryside: I don't shoot, myself, but as a target reader, the typical *Field* subscriber made for an interesting study. The magazine itself is a glossy monthly packed with the usual fare—buying guides, practical advice, opinion pieces, features, reviews—but its readership is drawn from a much narrower demographic than you'd usually get. Very affluent, very upmarket, very conservative (in its outlook and politics). But also fun-loving, irreverent, and self-confident.

A line I used to flatter the reader reads as follows:

I should mention this invitation is being sent only to those who fully appreciate the finest in all things, from guns to dogs, wines to fly rods.

It does several things at once. It positions the offer as exclusive. Not everyone is receiving it, so it falls into the same category as all those other luxury goods the reader either desires or possesses. The idea that the reader has impeccable taste is the core of the message and one difficult to reject as not applying to them. Finally, and in a very subtle way indeed, it suggests that in *not* subscribing, the reader would be "not quite the right sort." Given the aspirational nature of the purchase for anxious-to-fit-in hedge fund managers and the like, we felt this was a killer.

I once started another letter, to executives who made a lot of business flights, "As someone who spends a fair bit of time in the air, you're used to seeing further than other executives." Same idea with a twist, in that they *literally* see further, from 30,000 feet up.

In practice

- Flattery gives you an opening, but be subtle; despite Disraeli's injunction, troweling it on may be counterproductive.

- Use your common sense: poor people will be unimpressed by copy suggesting they have huge financial acumen. Call them careful with their money though and they're more likely to give you a hearing.

62 YOUR QUESTIONS ANSWERED

I'VE ALREADY TALKED about using questions to build rapport with your reader. There's another way you can use them in your copy and that's to create a Q&A section. Websites often have an FAQs (Frequently Asked Questions) page but they often miss the point, I think, in being unimaginative directories of actual problems and their solutions.

As you plan a brochure, let's say (but it could be a web page, sales letter, or ad), you may well have written a list of all your prospect's objections to buying from you. These are what I call the "what ifs." You can answer them in the body copy, sure. But you can also address them separately in a panel or box-out. This draws the reader's eye and the interview-style format feels comfortingly familiar.

The idea

From a small organizational growth consultancy

Because this one-man-band consultancy was working in a very new area, there were bound to be skeptics. Suggesting that business managers meditate at work, do breathing exercises and creative visualization exercises was definitely on the flaky end of the management consultancy spectrum, even in the boom years when this client of mine was flourishing.

So, we decided to create a set of typical questions—objections—that the prospect might have, in order to deal with them one at a time. In response to a question asking whether this was all a bit new-age, we referred to scientific evidence that the techniques being espoused worked.

You can also use a Q&A section to do some under-the-radar selling: what I call "stealth selling." The idea is that you continue to write benefits-laden body copy but simply by formatting it differently, encourage people to read it. This is not a con. You still have to be believable and your product still has to deliver what you say it does. That being true, your problem as a copywriter is holding the attention of your reader long enough to show them why what you say is beneficial to them.

Here's how you do it:

Your questions answered

Q: Isn't this idea just tricking people into buying something they don't need?

A: Not at all, it's just a way of attracting their eye to some truthful copy about your product.

In practice

- Make a list of some questions you know potential buyers would ask you, especially ones based on misconceptions about you or your product.

- Then pair them with the answers in a tint-box or panel formatted to look like a typical magazine interview.

63 ● HOW TO GO UPMARKET

THERE ARE TIMES when you want to go deliberately upmarket. Perhaps you're selling a very expensive product; or you're selling a cheap product to very expensive people. Either way, you need to strike that elusive tone of voice and style that reassures your reader that they won't be rubbing shoulders with the hoi polloi if they buy from you.

Preserving that sense of exclusivity is about more than using the word "exclusive." In fact, along with "exciting" and "unique," "exclusive" is one of the most overworked old nags in the language, repeatedly pressed into service and weighed down with expectations that it can never deliver.

The idea

From The Economist Group

I have written hundreds of conference promotions for this company, whose delegates are usually charged around £1,000 a place. So not cheap. But, for my client, still an average event in style, content, and delegate profile. When they decided to go truly upmarket, they did without delegate fees altogether. The pitch wasn't, "If you have to ask how much it costs, you can't afford it." It was more like, "If you have to ask whether you can attend, you can't." In other words, it was all about the exclusivity of the event. Called The Global Agenda, it convened (still does) small groups of extremely influential and powerful individuals. Not just any old CEOs but CEOs of the world's largest corporations. Plus Nobel Prize winners, leading academics, and very senior politicians.

So, an invitation-only event for very important people indeed. The language had to reflect the Economist brand, the unique (there's that word again) character of the meeting, and the participants' own expectations and sense of self-esteem, which we assumed would be high. Here is the opening from the invitation:

> Many speculate about the shape of things to come, but few speak from a position of authority. The corporate and thought leaders invited to take part in this roundtable have, more than most, the experience and insight to make such a claim.

Contrasting the many with the few leaves the reader in no doubt which group he or she belongs to. Referring to the reader in the third person plural—which breaks one of my own cardinal rules—works here, seeming aloof from the grubby business of direct mail selling.

I also deliberately used a slightly arcane vocabulary—"academia," "a crucible for new thinking," "alumni"—to reinforce the sense that this would be no ordinary talking shop.

In practice

- If you are going upmarket, aim for a higher register than you'd normally use—you get to break all the rules about short words, and simple sentences.

- Ask your designer to use a classical serif typeface, Palatino or Perpetua perhaps, with generous margins and leading. Buy the best paper you can afford.

64 USE PICTURES YOUR READER IDENTIFIES WITH

USING PICTURES TO attract people is as old as advertising, but you have to choose the right ones to make your copy work harder. Attracting them is one thing, getting them to read on quite another. Believe it or not—and why should it be so hard to believe?—people look at photos they can identify with. That often means human faces. Human faces of the same gender as the reader.

You can go further of course. If you're selling a business product or service aimed at CEOs, show some CEO-looking person. In other words, unless it's a software product, someone in their forties or fifties. If you're selling to parents, show a mum. (Yes, I know dads are parents too, but it's the women who make most of the purchase decisions.)

The idea

From a health supplements firm

If you were writing an ad aimed at persuading young men to buy protein muscle-building supplements, what picture would you choose? A buff looking guy with ripped abs? A close-up of a pile of the miracle powder that would give the reader muscles like *these*? A set of dumbbells with the caption, "Throw these away—you won't be needing them any more"? Any of them would be a great place to start.

Yet, following a long and not particularly honorable line of builder's merchants, petrol companies, and tool manufacturers, the makers of product X went for . . . a girl in a bikini, smiling winsomely at the camera. We can imagine the thought process quite easily (it wasn't much of a process).

> Writer: "We're aiming this product at young guys who want to attract girls."
> Art director: "Cool. Let's get a model to pose in a bikini."
> Both: "Yes!" They high-five. "Guys will have to look at the ad then."

Now let's listen in to the reader's thoughts as he flicks to the ad . . .

> "Coo, she's nice. I like her." Turns page.

Sadly, although young men—well, OK, men—love looking at pictures of scantily clad females, that's about as far as it goes. They look. They don't *identify*—crucial for making a sale; and they have no reason to read the body copy. (Which in this case ran to all of 25 words.) It's just another pretty girl.

If you're marketing bikinis, tanning lotions, or slimming courses to young *women*, this could well be the ideal picture (just don't make her too pretty).

In practice

- Illustrate your ads with photographs that show the product. That's what you're expecting your prospect to hand over their money for.

- Give your reader a same-sex face to look at: builders identify with builders not glamor models and may, just, be tempted to find out what *this* builder is pitching.

65 POWERED BY FACTS

Around about half-past nine on your first day as a copywriter, a graybeard will wander over to your desk and intone, portentously, "You know, features don't matter, it's benefits that make the sale." They stroll off again to suck the end of their pencil while dreaming of their "Best Screenplay" Oscar.

They're right, of course. Features don't matter as much as benefits. But here's the interesting thing. There's an "F" word that matters much more than "features" and can really turbocharge your benefits copy too. Facts. Your customers will be impressed by facts. They will be persuaded by facts. They will be emotionally engaged by facts.

The idea

From Porsche

Porsche press ads echo the original art direction of the Bill Bernbach ads for the VW Beetle when it was first launched in America. Big picture (of the car in motion—a step away from the original "Lemon" ad). Headline underneath (the correct position for it). Then the body copy. The headline is a benefit-free zone. Mind you, in luxury goods advertising—perfume, watches, couture—the benefit is inherent in ownership. "Makes you feel sooo good about yourself."

What it does have, however, is a killer fact. "One highly efficient sports car. The new 911 Carrera with Porsche Doppelkupplung PDK."

PDK is a new automatic transmission developed by Porsche with a double clutch (Doppelkupplung). The body copy goes on to explain just how this fact translates into more facts, about performance—crucial in the sports car market—fuel consumption (less so) and emissions (a nod to the green lobby as you splurge your inheritance on Stuttgart's finest).

When you write your own copy, dredge up as many facts about your product as you can. If you publish subscription products: newsletters, magazines, newspapers, or websites, tell prospective subscribers how many of their peers already subscribe. If you offer a service that saves businesspeople money, calculate and then explain—precisely—how much money they'll save. And over what period. If you offer some life-improving product or service, dig up some facts that prove it works.

You could even set your facts in a separate section of your ad or web page. Under a heading reading, "Ten facts about the new wonder widget that *prove* it's better."

In practice

- The key is research. Talk to the people who create the product you're selling. Find out as much as you can about it.

- Try to avoid bombarding the reader with too much information and too many numbers. Sometimes what you really need is a single killer fact that will convince on its own.

SELLING TO INTERNATIONAL MANAGERS

WHEN I WAS asked to write a mailpack for a business information service, the biggest challenge was connecting with international managers. The analysis is written in English, but many subscribers are non-native speakers. Add differences in culture, industry, seniority, job role, and interest and you have a tough brief.

The control pack featured wordplay and clever headlines. With no substantive changes to the product, the emphasis was on trying a different approach to the sales pitch. After a meeting with the marketeer responsible for the service, we pinpointed a few big ideas that would shape the copy.

The idea

From a large business information company

I suggested we abandon adjectives such as "authoritative" and "reliable" in favor of facts, evidence, and concrete examples. So, we decided to include copy that sold the reports as the product of an editorial process that no other company could match: the USP. We would flesh it out with profiles of key editorial staff and explain in detail how data were collected and checked.

And what of the international readership for the promotion? I ditched the puns and cleverness in favor of a straight explanation of how the reader would look good, reduce business risk, and take better decisions in less time. Cultural considerations meant that the word "gospel"—describing data quality in an early draft of the letter—was changed to "accurate." I also used the simplest language possible. That meant short words, and short sentences: in the letter, the average sentence was just under 15 words; in the brochure, it was just under 14.

Behind the benefits copy was a set of four psychological triggers designed to tap into the reader's deep-seated drives. *Fear*: of making a bad decision through being ill-informed, and the negative consequences that would flow from it. *Anger*: that some websites would be palming off unchecked data as reliable when it wasn't, so taking them for a fool. *Salvation*: in the sense that simply by subscribing they could remove worry and doubt from their decision-making. And lastly, *flattery/exclusivity*: that they would be joining a worldwide group of highly respected senior managers.

In practice

- Use the simplest language you can to ensure your reader is thinking about life with your product, not reaching for the dictionary.

- Remember, what you say is more important than how you say it: international managers (who are, after all, local managers from their own perspective) all ask the same question: "What's in it for me?" And they always will.

67 SKIP SKIP INTRO

OVER THE YEARS, I have developed a certain affection for a few types of copywriting. Long sales letters, especially if set in Courier. That quirky stuff you get on the backs of Innocent smoothies, Ribena cartons, and Ben & Jerry's ice cream tubs. And even Google Adwords, which approach the simplicity and resonance of haiku.

Yet, there are other classes of—can I call it copywriting? Not really but it'll do for now—that leave me puzzled at best and groaning at worst. Like all new media before it, the web has spawned its fair share of dimwit copy ideas, and one of the dimmest I discuss below.

The idea

From the wonderful www.skipintros.com

The other day I was researching content for a client's case study and out of the five websites they gave me to look at, no fewer than three had, you guessed it, a "movie" with the deathless phrase "skip intro" somewhere toward the foot of the page. I'm sure you've seen them: two minutes of silky/juddery/morphy nonsense, no doubt intended to lull you to sleep so that the dubious claims that follow won't be subjected to critical scrutiny.

Now, let's ask the owner of this website a question. Did you think I typed in your URL so I could watch a *movie*? Duh! I want information and I want it *now*. Only a fool actively erects barriers between a potential customer and his content. The playful folk at www.skipintros.com have this mindset parodied to perfection.

I think I know what's going on. The companies who pay for this type of website usually don't rely on it for sales. It's largely an exercise in self-aggrandisement, so the practice of Flashturbation is entirely in keeping with the garbled corporate nonsense that takes up the rest of the site. But then, hey, they probably send out sales letters that start "As a valued client" as well.

I have a suggestion for a more user-friendly line of copy on the home page. It reads: "Play pointless Flash movie that we paid a fortune for and are now desperate to have you watch." Then the small children at whom these animations are so clearly aimed could sit there all day watching zebras turning into photocopiers while the rest of us get on with some work.

In practice

- If you see web designers putting "skip intro" between your visitors and your copy, a) whack them with something heavy and b) ask them when was the last time they read a book that started "skip intro."

- If you are asked to take part in a web design meeting and it comes up, remind everyone that an anagram of "skip intro" is "irk points," which you will win from visitors.

68 SATISFY THEIR CRAVINGS

WHEN PEOPLE NEED stuff, they will buy it. Just don't expect it to be a particularly motivated customer. Life insurance, new wellington boots, a replacement wastepaper basket: they get bought but not drooled over. Contrast that state of mind to the one when they *want* something. *Much* better. If the want in question is some fundamental human need—sleep for example—it would take an idiot not to be able to connect with their prospects.

Much as people—marketing people especially, I have often noticed—claim to find selling distasteful, without it there is no buying. So being sold to is a good thing. And *if* you're being sold something you really want it's a fantastic thing.

The idea

From a nighttime nanny service

If you have children of your own, this isn't going to be a stretch, and if you haven't children, I still think you'll get it very easily . . .

What would it be like to go without a full night's sleep for a year? Or two years? Or three? Not no sleep. Just sleep interrupted every hour or two by a crying, no, make that a screaming, baby. Pick your own noun. Mine would be purgatory. Hell is shorter and probably more accurate. So how wonderful would it be if you received a mailing from a company promising to make this peculiarly horrible pain vanish, literally overnight.

That's exactly what my client was offering. Highly trained and qualified nannies who would sort your baby's sleep problems out for you while you slept. Here's some of the copy that tuned into these sleep-deprived, middle-class parents' nightmare . . .

Do you dream of a full night's sleep?

Remember those nights of unbroken sleep? Of waking when *you* were ready, not your little one? We can bring them back for you.

This is the opposite of fact-based copywriting—it's all about emotion. And sometimes it is the easiest to write—no need for AIDCA or any other mechanistic approaches. Your prospects might be frightened rigid by mounting debts; they might be consumed by wanderlust; their heart might race at the mere thought of a gastronomic tour of the world's finest restaurants. Where you can satisfy a craving, a want, rather than just a need, your job is immeasurably easier.

In practice

- As you plan your copy, look hard for the deep-seated cravings that your product satisfies. Just be careful how you phrase it: people don't like their more base desires thrust in their faces.

- Even if your product is a nice to have rather than a must have, if you can find a way to make it *feel* more desirable you engage people's emotions as well as their reason.

TAILOR THE MESSAGE TO THE AUDIENCE

69

THIS MIGHT SOUND obvious. You'd hardly use the same copy to sell to 20-year-olds as you would to 60-somethings would you? Would you? I bet you've seen examples where exactly that has happened. Or you find one piece of copy being used for a white paper, a policy report, and an ad campaign. Or the same language being used to appeal to customers, prospects, and staff.

It might work. It's just unlikely to. One of the first things we do as copywriters is try to understand who we're writing to. Grannies? Or kids? Business managers or nurses? Each group will have its own defining characteristics and we should be aware of those when we write.

The idea

From *The Times Literary Supplement*, a newspaper

Some years back, I was writing a lot of copy for the *TLS*: new subscriber acquisition mailings, renewal letters, house ads. And each time we had a very narrow target market. We characterized them, not unkindly, as 60-year-old Hampstead intellectuals. You know, blue stockings. Inkhorns.

Then, one day, we had a radically different audience in mind. Students studying English literature. You could, I suppose, think of them as intellectuals. But fairly green ones. It's a challenge getting retired people with lots of time on their hands to subscribe to a weekly newspaper full of densely written, erudite book reviews. But students? Come on! What could we do to break through the indifference barrier and reposition the *TLS* as a useful tool to help them with their studies? The answer presented itself almost at once. Drugs.

As I write this, the poster I wrote stares down at me off the wall of my office. Try to picture it. There is a *TLS* front cover taken up entirely by a photo of a huge tomato. The cover rests on a green spotted background. Beneath it is the headline:

Mind expanding substance

Visually it's arresting—it was designed to be posted on the wall of student bars and read from a distance. (A point you should always consider when writing posters unless they're for underground trains.) But it's the headline that carries the weight of the task. The druggy play on words was too good to pass up and is probably the only pun I have ever used in 23 years as a professional copywriter.

The *TLS* is not what you'd think of as natural student reading material: too many long articles, not enough pictures, and weekly into the bargain. But we managed to create a cooler image for the paper than it probably warranted by paying attention to the copy and design.

In practice

- Think about the language—vocabulary, register, keywords— your reader will be comfortable with and try to work within those parameters.

- Do not, under any circumstances, try to sound like a teenager. Unless you are one. In which case, well done for getting such a cool job so quickly.

GET A CROSS-HEAD

70

ONE OF THE biggest barriers to the sale is simply that your prospect doesn't, won't, or can't get to the end of your body copy. Maybe they don't even start. Research has shown that 80 percent of people who read an ad at all only read the headline.

And one of the biggest reasons why people don't read body copy is that it looks too daunting. They are confronted with a gray, forbidding slab of text with all the visual allure of a steel door. You may have written copy that *were it to be read* would convince a vegan to buy flash-frozen bison steaks. But they ain't reading. So they won't buy 'em.

The idea

From Inform Recruitment

Your best tool for breaking up long copy is headings. Specifically, those headings that run between paragraphs or groups of paragraphs, often, but not always, centered. I call them cross-heads and I use them all the time. The only time I avoid them is when I have a particular need to make a letter resemble correspondence. Which is almost never.

Inform Recruitment is a specialist recruitment consultancy that places qualified teachers, teaching assistants, and ancillary staff in schools across London. For head teachers looking for staff to cover absence the imperative is to find the right person, fast. The letter I wrote had the following headline:

> How to find the right cover teacher . . . and have them in school by 8.30 a.m.

Which was enough to get the head teacher to whom the letter was sent reading on, if not actually salivating. But knowing that most people see reading letters from strangers as a chore, I used lots of cross-heads to break up the text and make it look more inviting. Here they are . . .

- Teachers available for all Key Stages.

- Our three-point test for good cover teachers.

- Working in partnership with schools.

- 24-hour hotline answered by one of our team.

- Please call us today to find your cover teacher.

You can see that even without the body copy they do a pretty good job of describing the service and its advantages. There's a hint of a "secret sauce" in the second head—you'd definitely have to read on if you wanted to know what exactly this three-point test consisted of. But their most important job isn't to outline the pitch at all. It is just to make the text look easier to read. More user-friendly.

In practice

- For print DM copywriting, aim for three to four cross-heads per A4 page (letter in America). For an email or web page three to four per screen. For ads, one every two or three paragraphs.

- Keep cross-heads short; one line is best.

71 CREATE CURIOSITY

IT'S BEEN SAID that curiosity is one of the big psychological triggers or motivators. And it stands to reason. We *are* curious. It's in our genes. All higher primates start exploring their world as soon as they can. We puzzle over things. We love figuring things out. Almost as soon as they learn to talk, human children start asking, "Why?"

Which is excellent news for us copywriters. We can use our readers' natural curiosity to draw them into our copy. Because, wouldn't you know it, the answer to all their questions can be had for the price of the product we're promoting.

The idea

From *Personal Computer World*, an IT magazine

The readers of—and subscribers to—*Personal Computer World* (*PCW*) are well educated, mostly male, and mainly IT professionals. I was commissioned to write a direct mail letter that would be run as a test against the existing letter (the control). Like a lot of copywriters, I find the opening the hardest to settle on. Not because I can't get started, but because I can't decide which among several appeals will pay off with the best results. (Well, if I could, I'd be psychic and probably not writing copy for a living.)

I decided, finally, that male pride in being a technical expert, coupled with good old-fashioned fear of falling behind the pace, would form the bedrock of the letter. But how to start? Here's what I eventually wrote:

Dear Mr Sample,

I think you are like me. You're passionate about technology and you want the best you can afford. More than that, though:

That first six-word sentence does several things. It invites the reader to read it because it's so short. It implies that the rest of the letter will be easy to read. And, crucially, it piques the reader's curiosity. This was a two-page letter, so I assumed the reader would glance over the page to see who the letter was from. The Editor in this case. So the question my opening sentence plants in the reader's mind is, "*How am I like the Editor of PCW?*" It is also a subtle piece of flattery. By opening like this, I engaged directly with the reader's own sense of self worth *and* encouraged him to read my next sentence. In other words, I began training him to read past sentence breaks.

In practice

- Use curiosity as a motivator if you can, but be sure to link it to an appeal to the reader's self-interest. In this example, he was curious to find out how he resembled an authority figure in IT.

- A simple technique to get or keep people reading is to tell them that, "In a moment I am going to reveal to you the XYZ industry's dirty little secret."

MAKE YOUR ADS LOOK LIKE—AND READ LIKE— EDITORIAL

THERE ARE TWO schools of thought when it comes to ads. One says make it as vibrant as possible and keep the copy short because nobody reads long copy. (As this is often uttered by copywriters you have to wonder where they get their motivation to come into work from.)

The second school (the old school, if you will) says make your ad resemble editorial, since that is what people buy magazines and newspapers for in the first place, and write as much as possible. Why as much as possible? Because the only people who are going to buy from you are those motivated to do so, and they need and want as much information as possible before making their decision.

The idea

From Lynplan Ltd, who make sofa covers and sell them via mail order

When I came across Lynplan's ad in a Sunday supplement, I couldn't believe my eyes. Here, in late 2008, was a page ad clearly conceived, written, and art-directed by people who don't just want to sell more sofa covers (a laudable enough aim in its own right if that's what you manufacture) but who have bothered to find out what *works*. The ad (miraculously free of the ADVERTISEMENT header some newspapers and magazines insist on for ads with the temerity to comport themselves other than as nightclub flyers) begins with a headline enclosed in speech marks. It reads, "If you've just ordered a new sofa cover, don't read this . . . It will break your heart!"

At a stroke they call to the ad their entire target market, that is, people interested in buying sofa covers. Those who have will read because the curiosity factor is so high. Those who haven't will read because they think, rightly, they might learn something to their advantage.

The speech marks are important because they make the headline look like a real person talking. And indeed a real person is talking, as the ad carries a byline, "A special report by John Nesbitt." There follows a detailed account of Lynplan's products, service, even history as a family-run business started by the current managing director's father, a World War II bomb-disposal engineer. My favorite cross-head reads, "The 7 Things You Should Expect From Your Sofa Cover Company." I defy you not to read on.

I counted the words in the body copy and made it 745. Forgive me, Lynplan, if I missed a few. Top marks.

In practice

- Look at the articles in your favorite newspaper or magazine. Remind yourself that this is what you paid to read.

- Try adopting an editorial style for your next ad. Try signing it and writing it as if you were a journalist writing a story, rather than a copywriter writing an ad.

73

WATCH THAT HACKNEYED IMAGE

A LONG TIME ago, when I was just starting out as an independent copywriter, I wrote and designed a campaign for a client that had, as its central visual metaphor, an archery target with a bunch of arrows sticking out of it. The line beneath, if memory serves, ran along the lines of, "Keep your marketing on target." The results were OK, I'm pleased to report, but looking back I feel that this, perhaps, wasn't the most original idea in the history of advertising. *Mea culpa.*

Though I have moved on, plenty of companies are still stuck in that groove where chessmen, cheetahs, and, yes, archery targets get pressed into service whenever the writer thinks showing the actual product is too boring.

The idea

From me, I guess

The problem stems, I think, from a lack of either research or imagination. But also from a willingness to write in abstract terms about concrete propositions. You have a piece of software that enables sales executives to make more calls in a given week. That means that they're more likely to hit their target. "Aha!" says the copywriter. "Target!" And before you know it, our old friend the archery target is wheeled out.

Hitting your target is a metaphor. It doesn't feel like one because it's so widespread. Salespeople *are* given targets and are expected to hit them. (Or, puzzlingly, to exceed them. How can you exceed a target? You either hit it or you miss it.) Once we fall for the seductiveness of the low-hanging metaphor, its companion image can't be far behind. But there is an alternative.

If I were selling said sales support software now I would choose one of the following angles/images:

- A story about one individual sales executive, call her Sally, with details of just how much her performance improved, coupled to a quote from her and, yes, her picture.

- Screenshots of the software, maybe on a laptop in someone's car or on their cellphone, with copy explaining it's as mobile as you are.

- A picture of a shiny BMW with a caption, "That Most New Business Award just got a whole lot closer."

Prosaic? Possibly. But original, yes. Distinctive, certainly. Not seen a thousand times already by the prospect, definitely.

In practice

- Avoid any image idea that arrives unbidden in your brain. If you're finding them that easy to come by, so is everybody else.

- If you believe your product to be boring (I have heard plenty of people tell me this), consider showing it in use. Remember, the person who'll be buying it probably doesn't think it's boring.

74

CORRECT YOUR PROSPECT'S ASSUMPTIONS

WE ALL TEND to make assumptions about our customers. And probably the most common is that "everybody knows what we do so we don't have to tell them." It's true, most of our customers do know what we do. But they don't necessarily know *everything* we do. For example, I had been writing copy for corporate brochures for a good client of mine for years and then, one day, she said, "Do you know anyone who writes websites?"

I nearly choked. "I do," I managed. "Oh, great," she said. "I thought you just wrote corporate brochures." My mistake was in assuming she'd read my website. But who has time to do that? You have a supplier you're happy with, they do what you want them to, the end.

The idea

From Sportomotive, a sports car dealership

Just a half-mile or so from my house is a great little sports car dealer. As well as selling cars they also service them. Now, Sportomotive are Lotus specialists. (Do you know the playful-yet-painful owner's acronym? Lots Of Trouble, Usually Serious.) When we ran Saabs and, memorably, a classic Rover V8, I wandered in to ask them if they only serviced Lotus cars. "Oh no," said Cos, the owner. "We do all makes." "You should tell people," I said. "I'm not sure how many car owners around here know that."

Fast-forward a few years and as I sit here writing the book, Cos strides up to our front door and pops a flyer through the letterbox. Any excuse for a break, I think, and jump up to retrieve it. Here's the headline, a good one:

> Did you know we maintain all makes and models of vehicles not just Lotus?

I guess that's a pint or two of oil he owes me.

He reinforces the message with a simple array of logos for the makes he covers, ranging from Peugeot and VW to Jaguar and, because I guess a little cachet is always needed, Aston Martin. To get past the inertia barrier, Cos also offers a free 20-point Winter Check, a simple but effective offer and well-timed given that it's January as I write this.

In practice

- A simple little exercise is just to ask yourself, "What assumptions are our customers making about us?" Then correct them—you might sell more to them.

- Ask, too, what assumptions non-customers are making that prevent them from *becoming* customers. *Definitely* correct them.

A GREAT GOLF TOURNAMENT WITH A PRETTY NICE CONFERENCE ATTACHED

SOME YEARS AGO, London's Victoria and Albert Museum ran an advertising campaign that caused something of a stir among the chattering classes. The strapline was "An Ace Caff with Quite a Nice Museum Attached." Creating a stir was the aim as much as drawing crowds to the museum itself.

But where you have a very strong brand, you can afford to be a little playful like this. Your potential and actual customers don't really believe this is the way you see your business, it's just a bit of fun. It also sends a powerful signal about your confidence in your brand.

The idea

From a finance directors' conference

The conference I was promoting was a pretty serious event. Aimed squarely at what we have learned to call C-suite executives heading the finance function at big American corporations. When I was commissioned to write copy for the direct mail campaign, it was in its twelfth successful year (as conference marketing folk put it).

The briefing materials included previous campaigns, and I was surprised (being a non-golfer) at the prominence accorded to the accompanying golf tournament. But I guess this is where a lot of business gets done and my client certainly knew their customers' likes and dislikes. So I borrowed from the V&A campaign. I couldn't go the whole hog and write a headline that said:

> A great golf tournament with a pretty nice conference attached

But I did feature the tournament on the front page of the letter, with the lines:

> And don't forget the [conference name] Golf Tournament—an ideal way to relax, get to know your peers better, and enjoy some of that legendary Miami sunshine.

On the second page of the letter I returned to the sport:

> As a delegate, you also get free entry to the [conference name] Golf Tournament. At the Jefferson Country Club's breathtaking, pro-designed par 72 (7,416 yard) course, you'll play 18 holes of top-level golf. But you need to book now: places are strictly limited. Simply register now then relax—your FREE place at the Tournament is guaranteed.

We all knew that the golf would be a great inducement. And let's be honest, justifying it to the finance director was going to be a cinch: they *were* the finance director. We gave them rational reasons for attending in the form of business benefits. But I suspect the golf was the true motivator for a goodly chunk of the delegates.

In practice

- Don't overlook the fun elements of what you're selling. You could say "Buy this pen set for £12,000 and we'll throw in a new car free of charge."

- Make sure your prospect has enough intellectual reasons for buying so they can justify the purchase to *themselves*.

76 ACT LIKE A MAGPIE

MAGPIES ARE KNOWN for their petty larceny. They love bright, shiny objects and will cheerfully nick wedding rings, silver spoons, and trinkets from your house to decorate their nests. Copywriters should be a little like magpies too. Yes, it's great to come up with your own ideas, but not until you've had a good rummage through everybody else's.

This isn't me being lazy either. Pick your copywriting titan: all have borrowed freely from their forebears. The trick is to find a good idea, steal it, then adapt it to make it relevant to the product you're selling.

The idea

From a dozen or so great copywriters

When I started out as a copywriter, at the tender age of 22, I had no idea at all what was involved. So I did the only thing I could think of and went out and bought a bunch of copywriting books. Among them were *How to Write Sales Letters that Sell* by Drayton Bird, *The Secrets of Effective Direct Mail* by John Fraser-Robinson, and *Advertising That Pulls Response by* Graeme McCorkell.

I read them cover to cover, making notes and trying to figure out how to apply their ideas to my own job. Since then I have kept on buying books and my shelf now groans under the weight of a couple of dozen well-thumbed friends. Those I have donned the stripy sweater and eye-mask most often for include *The Solid Gold Mailbox* by Walter Weintz, *How to Write a Good Advertisement* by Victor Schwab, *Tested Advertising Methods* by John Caples, *The Adweek*

Copywriting Handbook by Joseph Sugarman, *The Copywriter's Handbook* by Robert Bly, and Drayton Bird's two books: the one above plus *Commonsense Direct and Digital Marketing.*

Stuck for headline ideas? Caples gives you dozens of formulae. Schwab has 100 headlines with a pithy explanation of their appeal. Need ideas for building a sales pitch for a web page or email? Take Bird's books and replace "sales letter" with "landing page."

Nowadays the fledgling magpie doesn't just have the local library or bookstore to raid. There are innumerable blogs, e-zines, Squidoo articles, and websites to filch ideas from. If you've got deep pockets and you spend enough time on eBay or Amazon you might even unearth a copy of legendary hardback *Reality in Advertising* by Rosser Reeves (that bloke wot invented the Unique Selling Proposition).

In practice

- Before you start chipping that lumpy square of rock into a circle with a hole through the middle, why not check to see what other copywriters have done?

- Copying another writer's words exactly rarely works. You need to steal the *idea* not the execution.

WATCH YOUR READABILITY

Copywriting quality is such a subjective area that many people flounder when asked to judge the merits of two versions of the same piece. Or of two completely unrelated pieces of copy. In direct marketing, print or online, you have response rates of course. But a lot of the time, the discussion takes place before the piece is mailed or deployed.

There are three main battlegrounds when arguing about copy quality. The first is seniority. "I'm in charge and I say it sucks." The second is experience. "We did this last year and it blew the control out of the water." The third is readability.

The idea

From a large organization that must remain nameless

I was hired to advise this rather bureaucratic organization on how it might improve the quality of its copywriting. In particular, they wanted me to look at their website, which ran to several thousand pages. (I didn't review them all of course, just enough to get a feeling for their style—and any problem areas that might exist.) The first test I ran, because the text looked unforgivingly long-winded, was to measure readability. To do that I used the Flesch Reading Ease test, which is embedded in Microsoft Word for Windows®.

Rudolph Flesch was an Austrian-born author, writing consultant, and readability expert. He wrote numerous books on the subject of Plain English and developed the Flesch Reading Ease test. It's a formula that uses the average number of syllables per word and the average words per sentence to calculate a percentage score. The higher the better.

To test my client's web copy, I cut and pasted a couple of hundred words from their home page into Word, then ran the test. Before I give you their score, let me share just three benchmarks from Rudolph Flesch's own article on writing Plain English. Consumer ads—82 percent. *Reader's Digest*—65 percent. *Harvard Law Review*—32 percent. Now for my client. Zero. Or, in other words, their online marketing copy was slightly easier to read than the American Internal Revenue Code but slightly harder to read than a standard car insurance policy.

The problem was twofold: lots of long words and lots of long sentences. Don't get me wrong: this wasn't incorrect writing in the sense of grammatical errors. Nor was it inelegant. It was just fiendishly difficult to understand. We began remedial work at once, chopping long sentences up into more manageable chunks (usually by finding semicolons and replacing them with full stops) and replacing long words with shorter equivalents.

In practice

- Get into the habit of checking the readability of your copy. It takes moments to do it and, to be honest, often not much longer to fix a low score.

- Aim for a Flesch Reading Ease score of 60 percent. That's Plain English. If you're writing for a specialist audience, you could go lower but remember, nobody *asked* you for this stuff.

78 SAY "HI"

IT'S GREAT WHEN you win a new customer. All that work on your e-shot, direct mail campaign, or sales promotion paid off. Your return on investment looks good. You've shifted some stock. Your database is now bigger by one. Well done you.

A lot of direct marketeers at this point go off in search of more new customers. But that's missing a vital link in the chain that could bind your new customer to you for life. Or at least for long enough to make sure you've sold them everything you could ever hope to. It's simply saying "Hi." And perhaps "thanks for your order."

The idea

From an international news magazine

Here's your customer, having just placed an order or sent you a check or their credit card details. Maybe the thing they ordered has arrived but maybe not. So there's this vacuum. You fill it with a welcome letter. In subscriptions marketing, which I do a lot of, it's the first stage in a process of getting the subscriber to extend their subscription. Because every profession likes to coin its own neat little phrases, subscriptions marketeers call it the "renewal at birth" letter.

For this news magazine, I wrote a letter that new subscribers would receive as soon as their order had been processed. Welcome letters shouldn't sound too professional or slick (though the absence of slickness itself takes some slick copywriting). Here's how I opened:

Dear Mr Jones,

I'd like to welcome you as a subscriber to [magazine title]. Thanks for your payment. You might want to keep the following pieces of information on file in case you want to get in touch with us:

The letter went on to provide the start date of the subscription, reinforcing in the reader's mind the idea that, yes, something will arrive soon in exchange for their cash; information on how to pause and restart their subscription if they were traveling; and a toll-free number to contact customer services.

In a welcome letter you can also take the opportunity to flatter the reader, suggesting that their decision to buy from you was a smart one. One taken by lots of other people, in fact. This helps dispel any lingering sense of buyer remorse.

Finally, I offered them the chance to buy something else. In this case, an extension to their original subscription period in return for a gift. A layperson's reaction is, "Isn't this all a bit too early to be selling more stuff to a new customer?" Er, no. This is exactly the right time to do that—just when they've done it once already.

In practice

- Whatever you're selling, prepare a welcome letter that you send to every new customer as soon as possible after you receive their first order.

- Keep the tone of voice friendly, warm, and conversational. Make them feel they've done something clever and offer them the chance to do it again by buying something else.

79 GRAMMAR *DOES* MATTER

In IDEA 10, I suggested that grammar doesn't matter. That what matters more is the underlying proposition you're writing about. But writing is key to the deal and since grammar, broadly, is to do with making writing intelligible, maybe it does matter after all.

There are lots of levels to grammar and, for lay audiences, certain mistakes will go through under the radar. If, though, you were to write "You didn't seen nothing like this never before," even somebody of the most modest educational attainment might tag the writer as a fraud. It's probably the easiest way to spot those phishing emails asking you to reenter your security details onto a bank's website.

The idea

From a large car manufacturer

I have a beautiful flyer in my Black Museum. Well, more than a flyer, really. It's a complex piece of cardboard engineering (that's a proper job, you know, I met someone who has it on his business card) involving glue, tab A into slot B, and all sorts of internal origami that ensures the insides appear simultaneously as you pull a thumb tab. Why was I telling you this? Oh yes.

Alongside the action shots of a very sleek, silver Brand X saloon is a shot of the inside: roughly 15 square yards of butter-soft cowhide with aluminum accents and carbon-fiber cupholders. Connected by a thin pale gray line to the ruched leather upholstery is the deathless line,

Not only bigger than before, our passengers now recline in electrically heated seats.

I still smile at the mental image this conjures up: bigger-than-ever passengers melting slightly as they squeeze their bulk into a leather-upholstered slow cooker.

If you're selling cheap goods where price is the only differentiator, quite honestly, grammar doesn't matter. People who want the cheapest lavatory paper really don't care whether you can write well or not. But if you're purveying high-quality merchandise to a more discerning customer, yes, it does matter. Your marketing materials, copy especially, should create an aura that attaches itself to the product and the whole buying process. Bad grammar says "wide boy" and sows seeds of doubt in your reader's mind. This book isn't the place for a discussion of "that" versus "which," the use of the subjunctive, or dangling participles, but they do matter and you should get grammar right.

In practice

- Keep your copy as simple as possible—this automatically reduces the chances that grammatical botches will creep in.

- If you're not sure of anything, check it, or have it checked. Reference books and proofreaders are cheaper than the cost of missed sales.

IN MY LAST book I took a fairly fundamentalist view of copywriting. Its only job is to sell. Avoid humor at all costs. Concentrate on the reader's self-interest. I still believe that, but maybe there's room for a little wordplay after all. Provided your copy is always drawing your reader further toward your goal—an order, free trial, meeting, or agreement—you can use any tool or technique that you think will work.

Like a lot of writers, I find wordplay irresistible. The English language certainly lends itself to puns, alliteration, assonance, and all sorts of linguistic monkey business. Done well it can entertain the reader and make them smile. That could be good if they associate the smile with the product you're promoting.

The idea

From Dec Marketing Company, an events marketing consultancy

When my good friend Andrew Dec asked me to write some copy for a postcard campaign to generate leads for his events marketing business, I started thinking about what every event organizer wants. Andrew works with conference companies, trade and professional associations: anyone who wants to run an event but not market or organize it. Clearly, for them, the objective is a full house. Nobody likes running a conference in a half-empty hall, a seminar with only the front two rows of seats filled, or an awards dinner where the gongs outnumber the candidates.

The headline I eventually came up with (across both sides of the postcard) was,

What if you ran an event . . . and everybody came?

It draws its inspiration from a 1960s anti-war slogan, "What if they threw a war and nobody came?"—which has enough cultural resonance even today for it to be adopted and adapted by lots of other writers besides me.

The key lies in making that small switch from "nobody" to "everybody." It's not a huge example of wordplay, but that's because I still cleave to my opening point, that it has to be in the service of the commercial goals of the copy. If you're confident in your abilities as a writer to uncover hidden meanings, spot links between concepts, and splash in the puddles of literary technique, then be bold and go for it. A reader smiling is probably still a reader reading. A reader laughing has stopped reading.

In practice

- When you're writing headlines, why not include a couple of more playful options in the dozen or so alternatives you draft for consideration?

- If you feel the urge to use words for comic effect, learn from the masters. Two reading suggestions: *Now That's Funny!* by David Bradbury and Joe McGrath and the Shouts and Murmurs column in the *New Yorker* magazine.

USE LANGUAGE YOUR CUSTOMERS CAN UNDERSTAND

IF YOU WANTED your four-year-old to wait for you before crossing the road, would you call out, "Darling, do you think, were I to recommend that you refrained from a headlong incursion into the thoroughfare, that you might attend me at the curbside?" I thought not.

Using an appropriate register for your reader is a pretty obvious way of making sure they can understand you. So why do so many organizations make it so hard for the target reader of a piece of copy even to figure it out? It's back to our old friend reader-centricity, I'm afraid (or rather, the lack of it).

The idea

From a service station in West London

When I lived in Chiswick, a leafy part of West London, there was a service station a mile or so away that had clearly become a magnet for drunks on their way home from the pub, looking for a coffee, a packet of fags, or a chocolate fix. Residents tended to complain vociferously to HQ about "noise nuisance" and it had obviously had an effect on the station manager. Right outside the kiosk was a beautifully printed and mounted sign on which were set the immortal lines:

> Out of consideration for our neighbors, would patrons kindly refrain from making undue noise or disturbance when leaving the premises.

Genius! That scores 38.4 percent on the Flesch Reading Ease test. Put it this way, that's harder to understand than the *Harvard Business Review*, a publication with which I feel sure the said patrons were unfamiliar. My question to the author is, do you really imagine that a group of "revelers," staggering noisily from a service station kiosk at midnight, are going to read a sign written like that, let alone figure out what the hell it means?

My translation would be something like,

> Please be quiet when you leave—don't wake our neighbors.
> [FRE score: 100 percent.]

In more obviously commercial arenas I still see plenty of examples of this long-winded style, where every big event is a significant development, and long-term plans are always strategic roadmaps. It makes no sense, literally, to dress up perfectly ordinary sentiments in Sunday best. And remember that everybody can understand Plain English, whatever their level of literacy or intellectual sophistication.

In practice

- Make sure, when you start writing, that you are using the sort of language you'd use if you were talking to your reader face to face.

- Read what you've written out loud. If you sound like a lawyer talking, you need to simplify it.

82 GET THEM NODDING

ONE OF THE oldest tricks in the sales book is to get your prospect to agree with you. Not on any earth-shattering subject like "do you want to buy this fridge?" but on an altogether less controversial plane. Classically, you suggest, on meeting your prospect, that it's a "nice day, huh?" Provided it isn't raining, you should get a noncommittal "Sure is."

But that "Sure is" is anything but noncommittal, because your prospect just agreed with you. Once they agree with you on a small point they're much more likely to agree with you on a big one. The trick is timing. You work through a few more easy questions and before they know it, your new best friend finds everything you say pretty uncontroversial. *Then* you ask for the order.

The idea

From a business-to-business mailshot

For the opening to a direct mail letter aimed at corporate managers, I adopted just such an old-school approach:

> Would you agree with me that running a business in Eastern Europe calls for a unique mix of skills? Skills observed in successful executives like you?

Kinda hard to disagree with that, wouldn't you say? Combined with some fairly obvious flattery, it almost forces the reader to say "yes." Which is all I wanted at this stage.

If you've figured out or researched what makes your reader tick, you have all the ammunition you need for this type of opening. It works for any kind of reader, and in ads, emails, landing pages, Adwords, or mailshots. Let's take a few examples . . .

- Parents: do you ever worry about your kids' education?

- Middle managers: people like us are the driving force in the business, aren't we?

- Home cooks: would you be interested in a foolproof recipe for wow-factor chocolate cake?

- Retirees: is it time seniors were given more respect?

- Competitive swimmers: want to know how to reduce turbulence?

Once you have their first nod, try to build on it with another one. Then you need a little body-swerve to bring them around to your point. "Well," you say, "in that case, you may be very interested in what I have to say next." Or, "Of course you do, we all do. And that's why I have developed this foolproof way of . . ."

In practice

- Allay your reader's fears that you're about to sell to them by asking them to agree with you on some inconsequential point.

- Or tap into their deeper motivation by suggesting something they hold to be true and asking them to agree with that.

DIG DOWN TO THE UNDERLYING PROPOSITION

THINK BACK TO the last time you opened a magazine. There will almost certainly have been a house ad promoting subscriptions to that magazine. In 99 percent of the ads I see, the copy essentially says, "Subscribe to *Aardvark Monthly* and save 75 percent." Or "Get this big bottle of Aardvark Scruffing Lotion for Men." Lots of copy about the offer, in other words, but very little about the magazine.

This offer-led approach is a valid one *if* you reinforce it with plenty of marketing messages focusing on the underlying benefits to the prospect. Without them, you attract people who just want to smell like Aardvarks and who'll desert you the moment someone else offers them a juicier freebie.

The idea

From women's glossy magazines

At the time of writing, there are two main copy platforms used to promote subscriptions to women's magazines in Britain. One, have a bunch of cosmetics. Two, get a dozen issues for £1. They're both successful at gaining new customers, but frequently disastrous for creating *loyal* customers. Incentivizing someone with a gift of perfume to make repeat purchases of what was an impulse buy in the first place seems doomed to failure. And, sure enough, many publishers in this sector struggle with attrition or, to use publishing jargon, renewal rates.

One of the publishers I work with explained that, frequently, renewals aren't the point. Where you depend on ad revenues for the bulk of your profits, page rates are critical. Buying circulation through incentives allows you to charge your advertisers more to reach them. She then went on to brief me to produce a series of letters that would connect with the reader through the underlying proposition. In other words, sell the product not the offer. Were there discounts and incentives? Sometimes, yes. But they were always subservient to the proposition.

The relevance to what *you're* selling? You may not have the luxury of being able to afford to buy customers at a loss to feed a second revenue stream. So make sure you sell the product based on its true appeal to the prospect, and only nudge them with your offer.

In practice

- Complete the sentence: Your life will be better when you buy product X because you will . . .

- Talk to long-time customers and ask why they bought from you originally and why they've stayed with you.

YET ANOTHER HEADLINE IDEA—USE "NOW"

FORGIVE ME FOR returning to headlines again, but given how much effort we all spend trying to come up with good ones, and how important they are, I assumed you wouldn't mind. It's true that appealing to your reader's self-interest is always going to be the most powerful foundation for a headline. But you can ramp up the curiosity factor, and the urgency, by implying that this is not just beneficial to the reader, but also new.

People like new things. New products, new ideas, new friends. So why not trade on this very positive motivation to add some luster to your copywriting?

The idea

From a health and safety consultancy

As a copywriter, I'm always looking for something unique about the product I'm promoting. You can always find an angle, but when it's a one-off, your job is just that bit easier. So when I was asked to write a mailshot to promote a new management report, I asked the client my standard question, "Is there anything this report does that no other report does?" The answer was, "Yes, it's the first report of its kind to provide comparable health and safety benchmarking data for every company on the FTSE 100" (that's an index of the 100 biggest companies by market capitalization listed on the London Stock Exchange).

The headline pretty much wrote itself:

Now, for the first time, reliable health & safety benchmarking data from Britain's biggest companies . . .

You don't just have to stick with "Now" either. Here are just a few of the ways you can introduce the idea of topicality:

- New . . .
- At last . . .
- Finally . . .
- Introducing . . .
- Announcing . . .
- You thought you'd never see it, but . . .

Like all formulae, you have to find a creative way to employ it. Suppose you had a miraculous health product that enabled people to see better at night. For example something derived from, oh I don't know, carrots—you could write something like, "Now, a new answer to poor night vision." Or, go a step further and ratchet up the curiosity factor: "New scientific research reveals the garden plant that could dramatically improve your night vision."

However you do it, give your headline a newsy flavor, something that makes your reader want to read on to find out the rest of the story.

In practice

- Even when your product is neither new nor revolutionary, if you dig down deep enough you will always be able to find *something* that gives you a news angle.

- If the product wilfully resists this treatment, create a new offer and focus on that.

IT DOESN'T HAVE TO BE A4, OR A5, OR . . .

I'D SAY ROUGHLY nine in ten of the direct mail pieces that arrive here at Sunfish Towers are packaged in DL or C5 envelopes. Open them and the contents are printed on either A4 or A5 pieces of paper. Ho hum. Even if the copy and design are working together to pull me into the pitch (which they frequently aren't), the very first message the pack sends out, long before it's opened, is, "Here's another boring bit of junk mail."

This is a golden opportunity, wasted. Consumers, business executives, professionals—whoever you're writing to, they're all so used to these off-the-peg packs that your words have to work twice as hard to get you a hearing. It doesn't have to be like this.

The idea

From a Sunfish client

When we were creating a new suite of direct marketing materials for this client, we wanted to penetrate the miasma of dreary direct mail so many executives get sprayed with every day of the week. So for one particular campaign, we used an undersized envelope. The letter was as tall as A4 but narrower, so it fitted inside the outer without a longitudinal fold. Instant cut-through.

Funnily enough you can often fit as many words into a smaller pack by judiciously editing the images and amount of white space in the pack. Or use a smaller brochure format but with more pages. However you do it, going smaller makes your mailing stand out simply because it's different. You know the adage, "Beautiful things come in small packages." It has some resonance here.

Or, go large. We once created a communications piece for a magazine publisher to let subscribers know that their subscription had finished a few weeks earlier. The mailer was an A3 flyer designed to look like a doormat. The "letter," reproduced on the photo of the doormat, which bled on all four sides, announced, regretfully, that this was all we could send Mr Subscriber this week because he had let his subscription lapse.

If you're creating a self-mailer, such as a postcard, get your imagination into gear and have some fun. Circles, die-cut shapes, more squares: yes, there's a cost involved, but when you look at the overall economics of direct mail, adding just a small increase in response rate will more than pay for any additional production work. And check out the range of stock envelopes available to you. There are plenty of square envelopes you don't pay extra for that can give your mailing a lift.

In practice

- For your next mailing, try a non-standard format. Test it against your control pack—you may be pleasantly surprised.

- Ensure your format is in line with your brand. If you're a firm of old-established family lawyers, an octopus-shaped mailer may intrigue prospects but ultimately not convince them you're serious.

CHEESE FOR CHRISTMAS?

IF YOU READ my last book or my regular newsletter you'll know by now I'm not a great fan of clichés. Threadbare, worn out, and well trodden, they convey little to your reader beyond the sense of having been here before. Except . . .

. . . except at Christmas. The rule for seasonal promos seems to be that you can't choose an image that is too cheesy. At this time of year you basically have seven choices: snowflakes, baubles, gift-wrap, Christmas trees, robins, starry sky, or holly. The best-performing house ad we ever created for one of our clients was, believe it or not, a clipart Santa, with the client's logo sticking out of the sack.

The idea

From Sodexo Pass, a service vouchers and cards company

Last Christmas, Sodexo Pass commissioned me to write a self-mailer for their Motivation and Incentives division, who wanted to market their multi-retailer shopping vouchers as staff Christmas gifts. My thoughts, naturally, turned to all things Yule, including carols, poems, visual imagery, and all the other cultural associations that are already floating around in people's brains at that time of year.

The copy platform was that here was an easy way to solve the problem of what to buy your staff as a "thank you" for their hard work all year. The designer provided the visual—a tangle of Christmas tree lights. My headline . . .

> It's that time of year again. Here's how to untangle the choice of staff gifts . . .

The theme continued on the inside with this line . . .

Light up their Christmas with SayShopping Pass

And this one . . .

Staff motivation isn't just for Christmas . . . here's a rewarding way to make it last all year

Smell that Gorgonzola. The point is, though, that people are more generous at this time of year and are, in my opinion, more willing to be entertained by marketing copy than at other times of the year. You see the same thing happening on Valentine's Day, at Easter, and on Halloween. But . . . there's always a but. Don't lose sight of the true goal of your copy. Which has to be to sell something. Yes you can use cheesy imagery if you're careful and it's done well, but forget to include benefits, overcome objections, or provide a strong and simple call to action and all is lost.

In practice

- If you can link your campaign or your product to appropriately seasonal copy and imagery, give it a go. People are more forgiving.

- Take out the feelgood factor this time of year generates, and I have my doubts about the cornball approach to selling.

87 GET YOUR CUSTOMERS TO SPEAK ON YOUR BEHALF

Not unreasonably, many of the people who read your copy are going to be skeptical of the claims you make. "Marketing speak" has become a pejorative phrase. It means, roughly, lies. So one of the ways to overcome your reader's skepticism is to present objective opinions from your existing customers.

Even though I am what you might call a seasoned pro, testimonials are still one of the first places I go to on an e-commerce website. And just think how eBay relies so heavily on feedback to maintain a sense of trust between buyers and sellers. Amazon, too, uses its reviews section for the same purpose.

The idea

From most of my clients

Even though they're an extremely effective and important part of the sales message, it's surprising how many organizations don't use testimonials. Maybe they don't have any. Or maybe they have them but just don't realize it. Either way, they're missing a trick. Not so my clients, for whom the sound of me asking "Have you got any testimonials" must get a little boring at times.

Why are testimonials effective? There are a number of reasons. There's something about the format of a testimonial that cries out to be read. There are the speech marks (inverted commas, if you prefer) for a start, which signal to the reader that here is a different voice, an *authentic* voice, speaking. Then there's the attribution, in other words, the tag after the testimonial that tells us who provided it. In an ideal world, it tells us who said it, and either where they live if you're selling a b2c product, or where they work if it's a b2b promotion. Testimonials also work well because you can treat them differently in design terms, pulling them out from the body copy, enclosing them in oversized speech marks, or even giving them a page or section to themselves.

How about getting hold of them? Three easy routes spring to mind. One, the best kind, unsolicited testimonials. These just arrive, unbidden, in your office, or in your inbox. Imagine having delighted your customers so thoroughly that they stop what they're doing *just* to let you know. Two, arrange your website so people can leave feedback. Three, ask them. You can write to people or email them, or hold focus groups, or send out questionnaires. It doesn't really matter *how* you do it, as long as you *are* doing it.

In practice

- Make it your priority to collect testimonials. You can never have too many. And once you have them, use them wherever and whenever you can—nothing reassures better than the disinterested testimony of an existing customer.

- Resist the temptation to edit them, except for length. If they don't sound like professional copywriters, so much the better: they aren't supposed to.

HOW TO DEAL WITH HIGH PRICES

OBJECTION HANDLING IS what salespeople call it. I do too. When you're planning a piece of copy you have to think not just of all the reasons why someone might buy from you, but of all the reasons why they might not. Price may well be one of those reasons. It's not necessarily confined to what we call premium-priced products either. If you're selling to the super-rich, then money really is no object. Their only objection might be that it's not expensive *enough*.

But in recessionary times, which we're in as I write this, or when you're selling to people who keep one eye on the budget (whether corporate or household), it pays, literally, to address the question of price head-on.

The idea

From *Time Out*, a listings magazine

How do you make the purchase of a magazine subscription look like small beer? The outlay isn't that great to begin with, maybe a few dozen pounds, but given that you don't get all you paid for until a whole year has passed, selling subscriptions needs some careful finessing on price.

For *Time Out*, I wrote a mailing letter in 2006 to win back former subscribers (lapsed/canceled in trade jargon). To convey the value of the subscription, I told a little story:

> And you have to admit, *Time Out* really is great value. On the way to work yesterday I saw a girl outside Starbucks drinking a grande caffè mocha and reading *Time Out*. You know

what? *The coffee cost more than the magazine.* And she paid the full cover price at a newsagent down the road from us in Tottenham Court Road.

I've used the word "value" twice already, and that's the key to resolving the price objection. Most of the time, price isn't the issue at all. Most people you're writing to can afford what you're asking. If they couldn't they wouldn't be on the list. But most people don't start out convinced that what you're offering is *worth* it. If they're not buying because of price, you haven't done enough work.

In practice

- The easiest technique I know to make something seem cheap is to divide the price by 365. Then you have the line, "For less than the price of your daily . . ." and fill in the blank with whatever seems appropriate for your reader.

- The other technique is to focus on the financial benefits that accrue to the buyer. If loft insulation costing £200 saves you that in two years, there's your objection overcome.

89 WHAT ARE THEY AFRAID OF?

WHEN YOU'RE SELLING, it pays to consider your prospect's most basic drives. There's a handful of them including fear, greed, sex, altruism, and curiosity. In copywriting terms, you're usually faced with a choice between fear and greed, in other words, your prospect is running away from something or toward something.

Gaining higher social status is a great motivation to play with, and it falls under the category of greed. Anxiety over debts piling up falls squarely in the fear camp. It's been shown time and again that fear selling is more persuasive then greed selling. Perhaps because, as someone once put it, "a man will fight twice as hard to hold onto a dollar as he will to gain ten."

The idea

From Octavian Vaults, a wine storage company

I came across Octavian Vaults while researching the world of wine collecting for another client. Imagine you're a serious wine collector. (Unless you *are* a serious collector, in which case, skip that bit.) Now, you've just invested, let's say, £5,000 in a case of 1995 Bordeaux premier cru. Where are you going to keep it? Under the stairs? I don't think so. In that nice limed ash rack next to the cooker? No. You need somewhere safe. Somewhere your investment isn't going to get knocked around, or spoiled. You need cellarage.

Octavian Vaults play, subtly but effectively, on the wine collector's fear that the precious bottles they've paid so much for are going to be either worth less, or, possibly worse, not worth drinking. The headline to the double-page ad in *Decanter* reads,

"Why wouldn't you want to store your wine perfectly in the safest place on Earth?"

And it's even signed by Laurie Greer, Cellar Master at Corsham Cellars.

On its own it does a great job of allaying, or starting to allay, the prospect's fears for their wine. The speech marks around it and the byline provide added believability, especially given that they're facing a picture of Mr Greer himself, looking every inch the safe pair of hands you'd want guarding your wine. The ad refers to their financial security, to the number of collectors who already trust them, and to the fact that this is "the only commercially accessible facility on Earth where you'll find [perfect cellarage]."

In practice

- Raise the specter of the thing your reader is worrying about, but do it gently. Make them too anxious and they'll turn the page just to be rid of the unpleasant emotions you're conjuring.

- Show them, quickly, how you can take their pain away. And provide every kind of reassurance you can that what you say is true.

"UNEVEN NUMBERS ARE THE GODS' DELIGHT." VIRGIL, *THE ECLOGUES*

ODD NUMBERS WORK. In creative fields, garden design, for example, or photography, we are often advised to group articles in odd-numbered groups. For some reason, a group of five plants looks more pleasing than a group of four, a group of three people in a photograph more interesting than a group of four.

I won't go into the theory here (save to tease you by saying the Golden Mean* divides a line roughly into thirds). The point is that it does work. Ancient masters of rhetoric knew the power of triads (groups of three) to influence their audience. Copywriters can, and should, do the same.

The idea

From the Bible and the French Revolution, among others

Faith, hope, and charity . . . liberty, equality, fraternity: just two examples of linguistic triads that have certainly moved masses. Great orators use this simple technique to add rhythm and power to their speeches. Think of Winston Churchill, asking for "blood, sweat, and tears."

When I'm writing copy, I like to think in terms of odd numbers, especially when writing lists of benefits. You could say, for example,

* The Golden Mean: a way of dividing a line in two such that the ratio of the shorter part to the longer is the same as the ratio of the longer part to the whole, roughly 1.6:1. In other words, two-thirds, one-third.

"There are lots of double glazing systems out there, but Acme Glass is the only one that saves you money, costs you less, and looks attractive in period buildings." Or, "Our customers know it's not just about service, it's not just about product quality, it's about a lifelong commitment to making their working life more productive."

The second example uses another technique I call reversal. Here you start off with two phrases that are linguistically parallel. Both use "not just" to lead up to the third, payoff phrase, which uses a different style to make the final, most sophisticated point.

When you're compiling lists of things, reasons to buy perhaps, or new features of product X, stick to odd numbers unless you're offering a top ten. For some reason this seems to buck the rule of odds. I said I wouldn't go into the theory, but one of the reasons odd numbers work is that they are asymmetrical, unlike even numbers. This asymmetry is visually interesting—it seems incomplete, like an unfinished story, and the unresolved tension draws us in. Maybe we, the reader, supply the missing item to make an even number.

In practice

- As an experiment, try arranging the next bulleted or numbered list you write first with an even number of items, then an odd. Compare them visually and read them out. Judge for yourself which looks and sounds more interesting and engaging.

- Try using an odd number in a headline, like this: The 7 copywriting secrets "they" don't want you to know.

HORSES BEAT CAMELS

91

It is said that a camel is a horse designed by committee. A little unfair on *Cameli bactrianus* and *dromedarius* but you can see their point. In copywriting, which you might imagine should be a solitary affair, committees have their sway too.

You can usually recognize the results of committee-driven copywriting. Lumpy where it should be smooth, ugly where it should be beautiful, plodding where it should be swift. And scraggy where it should be sleek. How does it happen and what can you do about it? I offer the following.

The idea

From a large multinational document and mail services company

Over the years I have written three or four corporate brochures for this large American-owned multinational. Plus presentations and web pages. They are, despite all the potential for camels, firmly in favor of horses. When talking the brief for the first one through with the communications manager, I asked her how many people would be involved in signing off the final copy. "Oh," she said, lightly, "not too bad for around here. There's me, obviously, plus our British and EMEA managing directors, the managing directors of our French, German, and Italian operations, the Global Head of Sales Development, and our Chief Executive." No pressure there then. What I should have done was run screaming from the room. But I'm a professional. Yes. So here's what I did instead.

I asked for the committee members who would sign off the final brochure to sign off the brief. This was important for a number of reasons. First, because I wanted to write a different kind of corporate brochure to the ones they were used to seeing. It would use storytelling techniques and an altogether warmer and more human tone of voice. I wanted to use real people from the client to tell their own stories. And I wanted it to read more like an extended direct mail letter with a defined call to action.

We had enough people on a conference call at the outset to get buy-in across the business. By getting this agreement from the committee before I started writing, it gave me the confidence to push ahead with a defined writing style for the brochure. I knew there wouldn't be calls for a different approach once I submitted my first draft. It was also important because once people have agreed to a copy approach they are less likely to disagree with its interpretation. I'm always looking for a reaction something along the lines of, "Oh yes, that's what we talked about in the briefing meeting."

In practice

- Find out who has the power to sign off your copy. Ask them to sign off the brief as well.

- Resist offers—or even demands—to rewrite your copy. (Result: camel.) Ask, instead, for people's *reasons* for their queries, then offer, sweetly, to attend to the changes yourself. (Result: horse.)

BEFRIEND A DESIGNER

A GREAT COPY/DESIGN team is a little like a songwriting team: one provides the words, the other the music that brings them to life. Get both halves of the equation right and your words get that sticky quality that embeds them in your prospect's brain. They'll be humming your jingle as they fill in their credit card details.

On the other hand, you, as the lyricist, might see your precious verses and chorus handed over to some hack with a tin ear. Now your copy jangles the reader's nerves and the easiest way to find respite from the pain is to junk it.

The idea

From Colophon, a small but beautifully formed design consultancy

Over the 20 years I have been working with Ross Speirs, the designer behind Colophon, he has taught me more than I have any right to know about good design. Not just what it is, but how to recognize it and why it's important. He's not one for awards ceremonies or industry citations but between us we've created promotions that have sold millions of pounds' worth of merchandise for our clients.

Here are five things Ross has taught me . . .

1. If you emphasize everything, you emphasize nothing. Making everything bigger—all the headlines, all the pictures, all the text—doesn't make anything more "impactful" [*Aagh!—Ed.*], just shouty. In fact, you can draw the eye by making a graphic element *smaller*.

2. Punters aren't interested in logos. "Make the logo bigger" is a fairly common request from inexperienced marketeers. Perhaps not realizing that punters are rarely interested in logos, they push the size up to the point that it drags the eye away from the selling copy.

3. Make it legible. It's common—as well as commercial—sense to set your type in a point size your reader can read easily without recourse to glasses. Ditto a typeface that makes reading easy, rather than a challenge. Slimbach, for example, or good old Times Roman.

4. Don't write to fit. Just because you can fit 750 words in Arial 10-point onto an A4 page doesn't mean you should. Unless you're writing a book, you need to leave your designer some room for images, forms, white space, direction indicators, call-outs, and so on. Less is more.

5. Keep things simple. Remember that the purpose of your copy is to sell, not to help your designer win a design award. Keep the number of typefaces, point sizes and weights, methods of emphasis (bold, underline, italic, contrasting colors), picture treatments, and general design techniques to a minimum.

In practice

- Make sure your designer works to the same brief you have, provided the very first line says, "Purpose of piece: to sell XXX."

- Horses for courses. If you're writing landing pages or blast emails, make sure your designer is an online specialist. Equally, for direct mail, make sure they know how to put a mailpack together.

93 USE PERSONAL DATA INTELLIGENTLY

I'M OLD ENOUGH to remember when mail-merging arrived on the scene. At a stroke, we were freed from our "Dear Client" direct mail letters. Now, we could address our customers individually (provided we had the data). But the rest of our copy was still pretty static. Occasionally we may have referred to our reader's company by name but that was about it.

That was b2b. In b2c copywriting, it was as if the whole world had gone from monochrome to Technicolor. Did you thrill as you read those breathless sales letters suggesting how envious your neighbors at 32 and 36 Railway Cuttings would be of your new block-paved driveway? I did. (It palled after a while.)

The idea

From the International Direct Marketing Fair, and other clients

When Reed Exhibitions asked me to write their exhibitor marketing campaign for the IDMF, the brief asked for copy that they could adapt to their personalized marketing campaign. Working with Lorien Unique, a dynamic content marketing specialist, the IDMF created highly personalized marketing campaigns aimed at each individual on their mailing list.

The idea extended to the visitor registration campaigns, with, among other formats, The Daily IDMF, a digital comic book-style promo that featured the recipient in the story, right down to the speech bubbles and picture captions. This is what I would call intelligent, not to mention extremely creative, use of personal data.

Another client has segmented their customers according to a range of variables including propensity to pay by direct debit, sensitivity to price, and engagement with the brand. Those three variables enabled me to write subtle variants on the same basic copy, addressing each segment's likely motivations and objections. More intelligence.

The possibilities offered by digital print open up still further creative avenues. For a client who themselves are digital printers and wanted to demonstrate the new technology to advertising and design agencies, I wrote a simple postcard. The image was a back view of a fairly androgynous model with their left arm extended, on which was a heart tattoo with the recipient's name. The headline? "Does your work make your clients feel this good about you?" A second postcard in the campaign had people (actually the client's own staff) writing the recipient's name with sparklers. Headline: "Sally, do your creative ideas make your clients go ooohh?"

In practice

- Everybody likes to be treated courteously and using your reader's name is a no-brainer. If you collect more information about them, try to use that too. But always think "How would *I* react if I read this?"

- Remember there's a big difference between personal and personalized. Calling your reader by their first name then writing boilerplate copy is more likely to annoy than engage.

94

START YOUR SENTENCES WITH AND. OR DON'T

I RUN REGULAR training courses on copywriting. And every time I do, there comes a point where we discuss some of the sacred cows of written (and spoken) English. Reactions from participants range from knowing nods to looks blending the deepest horror with a "You can't really be saying that, can you?" skepticism.

Put your hand up now if your teacher ever told you you shouldn't start a sentence with "And." OK, put it down again. The fact is, you *can* do this. A cursory search through any of the classics of English literature (or the editorial pages of *The Economist*) will throw up hundreds of examples. (This goes for "But," too, by the way.)

The idea

From a client selling mainly to older people

It's an interesting prejudice, this one. At my children's school, where I help out with literacy teaching, the teacher enjoins the children not to start sentences with And. Yet the books they bring home to practice their reading are full of And-headed sentences.

Here's why you *should* do it. As a device to add punch to a conclusion or additional point, starting a sentence with And is invaluable to copywriters. It also helps break up over-long sentences, which are far more of a no-no. I've done it all the way through this book. And I will probably do it all the way through my next one. But there are times when it's not a good idea, and that's when your reader will react negatively.

In practice, that means people of a conservative turn of mind; let's say people over 60. (Though even if your wanton slaughter of their sacred cows does put off one or two readers, the greater impact you give your writing will more than compensate.)

For one particular client, I had to sacrifice my natural inclination to pepper my copy with And. Their customers were almost exclusively older than 60. Not only that but they were of a bookish turn of mind and had very fixed ideas about "correct" English. So fixed, in fact, that had we mailed a sales letter with And at the start of a sentence, rather than placing an order, they would have written, longhand, to the company's managing director to complain.

Of course, anything done to excess is a vice, and beginning too many sentences with And or But will quickly grate on your reader's eye. But in moderation, it is yet another sharp little blade in your writer's toolbox.

In practice

- If you have a long sentence with a semicolon halfway through, or an "and" joining two thoughts, see if you can split it in two by starting a second sentence with And.

- Always consider your reader. Will they mind? Will they even notice? This matters more than your taste or my teaching.

95

BORING FOR WHOM?

IN CONVERSATION WITH a reasonably experienced in-house copywriter, I asked her what she saw as the downside of her job. "Writing copy for the same old product year after year," she said. "I wish I knew how to make it less boring." So I asked her, "Boring for whom?"

If *you* have ever been tempted to refresh copy for one of your products because it was "getting tired," ask yourself this question. Is the copy getting tired, or are you getting tired of it? In other words, what are the *results* telling you? Because that's all that really matters.

The idea

From a yearbook publisher

The copywriter I just mentioned worked for a yearbook publisher. They produced dozens of annual reference books stuffed with facts and figures on different world regions and industries. Sales were great—in their market, they were a known and trusted brand and their customers really needed this information. But because the product rarely changed, marketeers would arrive, write their first mailpack, then despair when they were asked to do the same again for the next book and the next and the next. Then do it all again the following year. But . . .

If the piece (ad, mailpack, HTML email, whatever) you're using is still achieving acceptable response rates—above your trigger for review—then you don't have a problem. Your customers obviously don't find it boring. Or at least, if they do, their ennui isn't affecting their buying behavior. So maybe you don't have to worry about the copy. How about applying that restless energy to list-research? Or to coming up with an irresistible offer? Or to holding a series of customer roadshows to find out what they actually think about your product (and its publicity materials)?

If you do decide that the copy is flagging—*genuinely* flagging—then you need to go back to basics. Looking at last year's copy and trying to pep it up a bit simply won't work. Given that it was probably a hacked-about version of the preceding year's effort, you're going nowhere fast. Here are a couple of ideas that might help . . .

In practice

- Get your hands on the product and actually use it. Pick it up and try it out. What does it do? Why does it do it better than anything else?

- Talk to people who bought it last year. Why did they buy it? How do they use it? What single thing would make them buy it again, even if every other feature were removed?

96

CREATE A QUESTIONNAIRE

PEOPLE *LOVE* BEING asked their opinion. It's one of the reasons market research companies manage to recruit members of focus groups or even just stop people on the street. And think of all the times you've seen questionnaires or personality tests in magazines. They're an editorial staple. So why not exploit this natural human foible (vanity?) in your copywriting?

The easiest way to do it is to write a questionnaire. You can have lots of fun designing it to look like a real one (well, in a way, it is a real one)—just make sure the questions (and answers) lead your reader to the desired destination: seeing the world the way you want them to.

The idea

From a computer magazine

Most house ads used by magazine publishers follow a very simple plan. Big photo of the incentive, or premium—variously, a bag of cosmetics, be-logoed sweatshirt, picnic hamper, golf umbrella, T-shirt, big bottle of perfume—huge headline advertising said premium plus percentage savings off the shop price, and a few lines reiterating the qualities of the premium.

For this computer magazine, the circulation manager asked us to come up with something a little different. The concept we suggested was a personality test. It followed the classic outline: first you answer a bunch of questions, with multiple-choice answers identified by letters. Then you add up your score. Finally you read off your score against a set of summaries to find out what or who you are. You know the sort of thing: "Mostly Cs—you are a business titan, able to take even the toughest decisions without blinking. You are destined for greatness and tragically under-recognized and rewarded."

The headline drew people in: "Could I ask you a few questions?"

We complemented it with a specially commissioned caricature of the circulation manager holding a clipboard. There were six questions, including: "When eating out, do you try the spiciest dishes?"; "If there's a ladder in your way, do you walk under it?"; and "Do you back up your files regularly?"

We arranged the answers using the three initials of the magazine's name and wrote summaries that always led to the same conclusion: subscribing to [magazine title] will make your life easier. We adjusted the benefits to reflect the "personality" the questionnaire had revealed: positive, cautious, or wild at heart.

In practice

- When you're writing your questionnaire questions, don't make it too long—remember the medium it's appearing in is advertising. (Direct mail gives you more scope, however.)

- Make sure the questionnaire has a *point*. You're not, actually, interested in their opinions at all—you want them to buy something from you.

GIVE PEOPLE A GLIMPSE BEHIND THE SCENES

People *love* getting insider information. For certain readers the idea that there's an elite group, somewhere, all having a wonderful time at their expense is sufficient motivation to stump up the cash for whatever you're selling. It's why headlines promising to reveal "the 7 secrets of professional manicurists" do so well.

Even people who *are* members of an elite worry that there may be a super-elite to which they are denied access. Perhaps because they are latecomers, or not of the right class, or from the wrong side of town. At every level of society, you have these anxieties about station and you can play on them to achieve your goals.

The idea

From an IT company

In the middle of a series of press ads for this IT services supplier, we decided to try something different. Rather than addressing the reader directly, in the second person singular—"you"—and talking about the usual benefits, we'd create a "fake" memo from the managing director to the marketing manager. The idea—conceit wouldn't be too harsh—was that, somehow, the memo had been printed in place of an ad, thus "revealing" the company's plans to its customers.

The memo read something like this:

> Dear James,
> Just wanted to remind you that our prices are going up next month. We should probably let customers know beforehand

so they get the chance to book next year's support contract at this year's prices.

Maybe a new ad? Or a mailing?

I'll leave the details to you.

Karen

The ad was designed to look like an internal memo, and set off-center against what appeared to be a normal page of editorial.

Opposite the ad we ran a bound-in insert with a straight presentation of the deal on offer and a booking form.

The results were good, better than the control. I guess people just liked the idea that someone had goofed and they could take advantage of this little piece of insider information. Even though it was a deal we could have presented in a straight ad, it just looked more interesting this way.

In practice

- If you decide to try this approach, make sure you nail the internal tone of voice. Imagine you're recording a meeting then just type up what you overheard.

- You could even create a little giveaway based on giving the recipient the inside track. Use words such as "revealed," "exposed," or "discovered."

98 TAP INTO PEOPLE'S ASPIRATIONS

I'M AN ADVOCATE of long copy. But there are certain products and markets where you really don't need to say very much. Think of luxury goods: watches, cosmetics, fast cars, couture. The ads you see consist almost entirely of an achingly beautiful shot of product X, often worn/posed next to an equally drop-dead gorgeous model. Maybe even a celebrity.

How many words do you get? A dozen? Three? Just the product name? In the world of aspirational marketing, you really don't need to spend hours describing the benefits of your product. It's there, flashing on and off in your reader's brain: "You too could be one of the beautiful people. If you buy this thing."

The idea

From a Swiss watch company

Two men stare out of the page at you. They are clearly father and son. The older of the two is immaculately groomed. He wears an expensive-looking suit and crisp white shirt (though no tie). Mid-forties and clearly in good shape, he has a confident, vaguely flirtatious smile that says, "I have it all. But that's cool. I don't need to shout about it." The younger of the pair also has lovely hair. He wears what looks like a cashmere sweater and a similarly confident smile. His says, "I don't have to worry about much in life. Can you imagine how great that feels?"

The copy runs to exactly 16 words on a full-page ad. It suggests (I'm paraphrasing) that you don't really ever own this watch. You are just holding it in trust for your children.

The ad drills down to a basic human motivation: wanting to gain higher social status. The whole premise is that by buying this watch (and a very nice pair of accompanying cufflinks) you are becoming the sort of person who has family traditions and inherited wealth.

People aspire to all sorts of things. Executives aspire to be promoted. Musicians aspire to win prizes for their playing. Parents aspire on behalf of their children. Does your product help them achieve their aspirations? If it does, you have a golden lever you can pull with your copy. The aim is to achieve a tone of voice that suggests that they are well on their way and with the extra little help they get from your product, those aspirational gates will swing wide open and admit them.

In practice

- One technique you can use is to cite the number of people just like your reader who are already benefiting from your product.

- Another is to relate the success stories of a few of your customers, with specific details of just how much money, prestige, or fame they have acquired as a result.

FOLLOW THE LAW OF GRAVITY

If Isaac Newton had been a copywriter, the apple that hit him on the noggin might have suggested the idea of reading gravity, rather than boring old Earth gravity. It's an interesting theory, borne out by eye-tracking research, that suggests there is a natural order in which people read ads, brochures, or web pages.

It goes like this: picture, caption, headline, subhead, body copy, coupon, logo. It's called reading gravity because the eye travels downward on the page, taking in each element in turn. You can turn this to your advantage or you can ignore it and force your reader to perform cognitive gymnastics as they try to decipher your copy.

The idea

From Streetwise Publications

Do you have a driving license? How fond of it are you? Would you like to know how to protect it—from speeding points, fines, or even confiscation? Streetwise Publications publish a guide that promises to do just that. I won't give you the sales pitch—that's their job. But as a piece of advertising that conforms to reading gravity, they've nailed it.

The mono ad has, at the top, a grainy photo of a policeman aiming a radar gun at, we assume, a speeding motorist. The headline next to it reads, "Drivers—Here's the Insider Information the Police Don't Want You to Have!"

It's a lulu. It identifies the target reader, uses our new best friend, the concept of insider information, and has speech marks to suggest it's a real person talking. It's bracketed by a teaser reading, "Outcast Traffic Cop Says . . . 'Protect Your License Today!'" and a subhead reading, "What Every Driver Must Know . . . Before It's Too Late!" (Not sure about all those exclamation marks, but maybe for this market they work.)

Then you have the body copy, two columns of six-point type with cross-heads to break it up. There's a bullet-point list, a panel listing press comments on the guide, two testimonials, and a "90-day cast iron money back guarantee certificate." Top marks for the copy on that last one. Finally, the order form, headed "Return this 90-Day Risk-Free Trial Now!" They've even turned the source code into a logo based on the silhouette of a traffic camera.

In practice

- You don't have to follow the principles of reading gravity. Lots of ads don't. Just be aware that the more obstacles you put between your reader and their comprehension of your copy, the less likely they are to respond.

- Avoid breaking columns of type with pictures. Readers will almost never read the second half of the column.

100 GET TO KNOW PEOPLE

IF YOU WANT to be a great copywriter, you will, naturally, want to read all the great books that have been written about copywriting, advertising, selling, and marketing over the last 100 years or so. Don't worry: it's not such a daunting list; most of the books written during that period on these subjects are not great.

But reading about copywriting is only part of the story. The real knowledge you need, the knowledge that will take you further than any book can, is what you can find out about people. Customers, prospects, readers, audiences: whatever you call them, these are the individuals you need to understand and relate to if you are going to sell to them. And let's remember, selling is what you—and I—do for a living.

The idea

From David Ogilvy

I thought it would be a fitting tribute to one of the twentieth century's greatest copywriters and advertising men to finish this list of ideas with one inspired by a remark of David Ogilvy's. When a young copywriter at his agency, Ogilvy & Mather, wanted to use a highfalutin word—"facilitate" maybe or "utilize"—he'd tell them to get on a Greyhound bus to Idaho and stay there for a week. "If you hear any of the people there using that word, you can use it too," Ogilvy would finish.

One of the best ways I have found to understand how other people use language is simply to talk, and listen, to them myself. Of course, depending on where you live, you may have to travel a little. When

I began working as an independent copywriter, I lived in a chi-chi enclave of West London. Our neighbors all had high-flying jobs in finance, the media, and the law. (The irony of the fact that we all lived in refurbished brewery workers' cottages did not escape us.) It gave me plenty of insights that I was able to use in my b2b work, but represented a very narrow cross-section of society. Now I live in Salisbury and rub shoulders with all sorts of people doing all sorts of jobs. Much easier.

However *you* do it, you need to develop an ear for the way people talk. Especially if you write for b2b markets, where there seems to be a common assumption that businesspeople spend their lives talking about significantly upgraded emoluments when they mean a big pay rise.

In practice

- Be curious about people. They should be your life's work. Every time you start writing a piece of copy, there's going to be a human being at the other end. Not a target market, audience segment, or demographic. A person.

- Read widely. Tabloid as well as broadsheet newspapers. Business magazines as well as glossies. Literature and poetry as well as business books. And listen to the way people speak. Develop an ear for the rhythms and inflections of everyday speech.

AFTERWORD

Rereading this book in manuscript form, it struck me that many of the ideas could be interpreted by an outside observer as being somewhat cynical. There's a lot of talk about playing on your reader's emotions and basic drives. About how people are driven by ignoble motives and what you, as a copywriter, can do to exploit these to sell stuff. I guess, though I like to believe the best of people, there's a part of me that is, if not outright cynical, at least a little wary of the reasons people give for acting in a certain way.

It's only natural that we should want to present our actions in a positive light. It's as if we have our own internal PR department, issuing press releases that always place a positive spin on our motives and our behavior. But is wanting to look good in front of one's contemporaries really such a sin? Is a desire for material things really something we need to worry about? Is a need for praise or flattery up there with pulling the wings off flies? I don't think so. We are who we are, and those of us who make our living as copywriters ignore all that at our peril.

ACKNOWLEDGMENTS

Many of the ideas in this book have come from projects I've worked on for my clients. I would like to thank all of them for their generous permission to use their campaigns as examples of great copywriting. Other ideas have been inspired by great copywriting, and occasionally design, that I have had nothing to do with but still respect hugely. To those companies and copywriters I would also like to extend my thanks.

Once again I have found it an educational and inspiring process to work with Martin, Pom and the team at Marshall Cavendish. Their advice, guidance, and friendship have made writing this book as much a pleasure as a job of work.

Finally, I would like to say a big thank you to my wife, Jo, and my sons, Rory and Jacob, whose patience when Daddy was hammering away at the keyboard will, I hope, be repaid when this book appears in print.

ALSO BY ANDY MASLEN

Write to Sell
The ultimate guide to great copywriting

How do you persuade someone to buy from you just by writing to them?
What does effective copywriting look like—and sound like?
***Write to Sell* has the answers.**

Read this book and you'll learn:

- The confidence and the skills to write better copy, faster.
- New ways to gain readers' attention, respect and trust.
- Hints and tips on turning selling skills into copywriting skills.
- Simple techniques to improve the readability of your copy.
- The impact of design and layout on copywriting.
- The meaning of good written English—the rules you must follow, the rules you can safely ignore.

Write to Sell is a guide to the *practice* of great copywriting—not just the theory. Checklists, exercises and mnemonics give you the tools to craft better copy. "Case notes" and concrete examples show you the difference between what works and what doesn't. Clear and concise, this is the copywriter's manual. Don't start writing without it.

ISBN 978-0-462-09975-0 / £9.99 PAPERBACK

FORTHCOMING FROM ANDY MASLEN

The Copywriting Sourcebook
**How to write better copy, faster—for everything from
ads to websites**

It's OK knowing the theory, but when it's 9.00 am and you've just been
given until lunchtime to write copy for a new sales email, landing page,
press ad or brochure, what you really need is a shortcut.

This book gives you a set of explicit, practical, step-by-step guidelines that
will help you write better copy, faster, for a wide range of formats, both
online and offline.

Seven things this book does for you:
1. Helps you achieve sales, marketing and commercial goals.
2. Gives you easy-to-follow advice on the right way to write copy.
3. Provides real-world examples of different copywriting styles and tones
   of voice.
4. Allows you to write better copy, faster.
5. Takes the stress out of planning and writing any type of marketing or
   sales copy.
6. Shows you shortcuts for beginnings, middles and ends.
7. Explains how a professional copywriter goes about his work.

The Copywriting Sourcebook takes the grind out of planning and writing
almost any type of copy by providing expert advice on the best layouts,
approaches and styles to suit everything from an email subject line to a
case study, a direct mail letter to a website. You can write copy without
it—but you'll take longer. Why take the risk? Buy the book instead.

ISBN 978-0-462-09974-3 / £14.99 PAPERBACK
PUBLICATION DATE: JANUARY 2010

OTHER 100 GREAT IDEAS

100 Great Business Ideas
From leading companies around the world
Jeremy Kourdi

Know how to prepare a deep-dive prototype? How's your social networking? And are you up to speed in your psychographic profiling and vendor lock-in procedures?

In the world of business, new ideas and energy are needed constantly—in many ways and at varying times—to ensure success. This book contains 100 insightful and useful business ideas that will help you succeed.

Written in a stimulating and flexible way, *100 Great Business Ideas* contains ideas with proven power and potency that actually work. The ideas are varied, interesting, and thought-provoking, and some of the best ideas used in business. Some are simple—sometimes almost embarrassingly so—while others are based on detailed research and brilliant intellect.

If you have a restless desire and the energy to do well and stay ahead of the competition and a willingness to experiment and take a risk, this book will inspire you to find out more or develop your thinking along new, creative lines, generating brilliant ideas for the future.

ISBN 978-0-462-09960-6 / £8.99 PAPERBACK

OTHER 100 GREAT IDEAS

100 Great Marketing Ideas
From leading companies around the world
Jim Blythe

**Do you know how to use promotional gifts that really promote?
Do you have a startling brand? Do you know how to discourage
the customers you *don't* want? Or even *how* to spot them
coming?**

Marketing moves fast—competitors come up with new ideas to
steal your business every day, so you need to stay ahead of the
game. This book can help! Written in an engaging and lively
manner, it gives you 100 ideas from real companies, ideas that
have been tried and tested. The ideas are thought provoking
and adaptable to most businesses—some are no-brainers
(which, nevertheless, are under-used), while others are subtle
and surprising.

Whether you are running a small business of your own,
working in marketing for a big company, or advising others,
this book will be an invaluable addition to your briefcase.

ISBN 978-0-462-09942-2 / £8.99 PAPERBACK

OTHER 100 GREAT IDEAS

100 Great PR Ideas
From leading companies around the world
Jim Blythe

Do you know how to turn a crisis into a triumph? Can you write a press release that gets you thousands of pounds worth of free publicity? Do you know how to hijack your competitors' PR and turn it against them?

This book can help! PR is exciting, it is essential, and it is easy to do—once you know how. Thousands of companies use PR to generate free publicity, to win over customers, to defuse criticism and potential threats from governments, and to put their name in the public eye. This book gives you 100 ideas from real companies, ideas that have worked time and time again to create the right impression.

Written in a lively, engaging style, this book gives you the ammunition you need to take the fight to the enemy. Whether you are running a small business or work for a major firm, or whether you are new to PR or have been in the business for years, this book has something for you.

ISBN 978-0-462-09949-1 / £8.99 PAPERBACK

100 Great Sales Ideas

From leading companies around the world
Patrick Forsyth

Do you "climb the stairs" to find new clients? Do you have a spoken logo? And how do you cope when you meet that prospect you just can't get along with?

Selling—the personal interaction between buyer and seller—is a key part of the overall marketing process. However much interest other marketing has generated, selling must convert that interest and turn it into action to buy. In today's market a key issue is to differentiate, to ensure your approach sets you apart from competition. A creative attitude to sales activity is even more important when faced with difficult markets or economic times.

Selling success can be made more certain if you adopt an active approach, understand the way it works, and deploy the right techniques in the right way. This book will help you achieve that success by providing a resource to assist the continuous process of analysis and review that is necessary to create sales excellence.

100 Great Sales Ideas is a book to dip into rather than read all in one sitting. The book contains 100 self-contained sales ideas from companies as varied as Raffles Hotel (Singapore), Sony and Amazon, with observations from Cathay Pacific Airways and Waterstone's bookshops, among others. As the author, Patrick Forsyth, states: "One new idea may take you a step forward in terms of results and customer satisfaction; a steady stream of them will secure your future."

ISBN 978-0-462-09961-3 / £8.99 PAPERBACK

OTHER 100 GREAT IDEAS

100 Great Time Management Ideas
From leading companies around the world
Patrick Forsyth

Do your priority tasks really get priority? Are you constantly interrupted, and do you find fire-fighting a necessity? Or do you see time as a resource that can be organized to maximize your effectiveness, and do just that? Really?

Your personal productivity and effectiveness help determine your level of success. Yet sometimes, the sheer number of things to do and the pressure and chaos that may pervade the workplace can overwhelm. The road to hell may be paved with good intentions, but so, too, is the road to effective time management.

Using your time effectively can transform your work patterns, performance and results, and the job satisfaction you get along the way. Time management is also a career skill, one that influences not just job success, but whole career success, too. Yet it can be difficult to achieve, and success is in the detail.

100 Great Time Management Ideas is a book to dip into rather than read all at one sitting (a fact that already makes it time effective!). The book contains 100 self-contained ideas to improve your management of time; all are proven, practical, and used by successful executives and managers around the world. As the author, Patrick Forsyth, says, "One new idea may positively influence how you work; here, it is no exaggeration to say that a steady stream of ideas can revolutionize it."

ISBN 978-0-462-09943-9 / £8.99 PAPERBACK